A Conversation with an Atheist

An ancient, reasoned and radical approach to knowing God

A Conversation with an Atheist

An ancient, reasoned and radical approach to knowing God

Daniel McKenzie

MANTRA
BOOKS

Winchester, UK
Washington, USA

JOHN HUNT PUBLISHING

First published by Mantra Books, 2023
Mantra Books is an imprint of John Hunt Publishing Ltd., No. 3 East Street, Alresford
Hampshire SO24 9EE, UK
office@jhpbooks.com
www.johnhuntpublishing.com
www.mantra-books.net

For distributor details and how to order please visit the 'Ordering' section on our website.

ISBN: 978 1 80341 226 9
978 1 80341 227 6 (ebook)
Library of Congress Control Number: 2022906039

A CIP catalogue record for this book is available from the British Library.

Design: Matthew Greenfield

UK: Printed and bound by CPI Group (UK) Ltd, Croydon, CR0 4YY
Printed in North America by CPI GPS partners

We operate a distinctive and ethical publishing philosophy in
all areas of our business, from our global network of authors to
production and worldwide distribution.

Contents

To my mother and father

Samsara: An exploration of the forces that shape and bind us
ISBN-10: 178904894X
ISBN-13: 978-1789048940

The Wisdom Teachings of the Bhagavad Gita
ASIN: B087MXW7L8

The Broken Tusk: Seeing Through the Lens of Vedanta
ASIN: B07KS2WVRN

To read more by Daniel McKenzie,
visit www.TheBrokenTusk.com

*This eternal yoga I taught to Vivasvan, Vivasvan taught it to Manu,
and Manu taught it to Ikshvaku. Thus handed down from one
to another, wise kings knew it. But with the lapse of time,
O destroyer of enemies, it has been lost to the world.*

Bhagavad Gita (4:1–2)

Prologue

"It annoys me when people bring up the notion there is a God. The whole debate around whether or not God exists is a nonstarter for me. Why believe in God?" questioned the atheist.

"Right. Why believe in God when you can *know* God?" replied the sage.

"Because there is no God to know!" the atheist shot back.

"To know God, you need God-knowledge. God doesn't make sense as a belief because by saying God is a belief, you're stating that God may or may not exist. All beliefs lack certainty. But when people say they don't believe in God it's usually the biblical God they're referring to. In other words, they are saying they don't believe in a 'Big Daddy' who sends people to heaven or hell depending on how many 'Our Fathers' they had recited." He added, "Oh, not to mention, God is pretty unpopular these days considering all the violence, confusion and corruption he has inspired. So to understand God, you need to clean the slate and start from scratch."

Unsatisfied the atheist responded, "Why should I even care?"

"Because in spite of all the religious baggage, understanding God is really about understanding the world. When you understand God, you understand that everything is the way it is and couldn't be otherwise. God isn't just some bedtime story to comfort you when life doesn't give you what you want. God is a part of life's equation, because it's really hard to formulate who you are and what the world is without knowing God." He continued, "Look, let me try to define it in a way that makes sense to your twenty-first-century tuned intellect: What is it that brought you into this world?... and don't tell me it was your mamma because your mamma has no idea how to biologically create a human being! What is it that right now is circulating your blood, telling you that you're hungry, and putting thoughts

1

in your head? What is it that's growing everything — the grass, the flowers, the trees, and the hair on your head?"

"Um, nature?"

With a gentle smile the sage answered, "Okay. For now, let's say nature is the effect and God is the cause. God is responsible for all the objects including you and me. In short, God is everything. Like a spider spinning its web, God is the intelligence, the energy and the material needed for creation."

"Sounds like more 'Big Daddy' to me," remarked the atheist.

"But God isn't an old bearded man doling out rewards and punishments," objected the sage. "God isn't even a person with human qualities. God is a principle, like gravity. In other words, God is impersonal. God is only in charge of rewards and punishments in so far as you follow *dharma*."

"And how do you define dharma?" asked the atheist.

"Dharma is the laws governing our experience — namely, the physical, psychological and moral laws. Physical laws exist so that fire is always hot and sugar is always sweet. Psychological laws exist so that certain circumstances, like experiencing love leave the mind peaceful, while others, like violence leave it agitated. Moral laws exist so that lying, stealing or hurting others feels wrong, and being helpful, cheerful or showing compassion feels right," the sage explained. "While we all intuitively understand these universal laws, very few people understand that to live a relatively peaceful life all you need to do is follow them! Look, dharma basically comes down to the following: (1) respect nature (2) mind your thoughts and (3) don't be a jerk!"

"And *karma*?"

"Good question. Karma shows whether or not nature—God—is currently on your side. It's like this: Go against dharma and nature will rub you the wrong way. It will cut you down and make you feel the pain. Go *with* dharma and for the most part, it's smooth sailing! This is why it's good to know God, because without God-knowledge you're a rudderless ship. In the end, God isn't watching you. God is just handing out the results of your actions. Again, it's all impersonal. The rules are already built into the system."

"What system?"

"The field of experience, the universe, the cosmic order... *this!!!*" the sage said with enthusiasm.

"Okay, so if we maintain that God or nature exists and that creation is governed by laws, then what created God? Oh, and please don't tell me it's turtles all the way down."

"Okay, let's see if you can follow the logic. Through an empirical process we can show that the source of everything is unborn, changeless, limitless, non-dual awareness. In other words, we are able to show that everything comes out of and resolves back into awareness."

"You'll need to unpack that for me," said the atheist.

"For now, let's assume that all experience is non-dual because without non-duality 'this' doesn't add up, in spite of what science says. According to science, the universe is random, its origin was an explosion that came out of nothing, and consciousness evolved from some dead matter. Now that's a bit of a stretch even for most scientists, so hear me out. From a person's point of view, strip away the body-mind, every limb, every part that you call 'me' and you have just awareness — the essence of who you are. I don't have to ask you if you're conscious because it's obvious. The fact that 'I am' is self-evident. From God's point of view, take away all of God's stuff, everything in the universe, and you also have just consciousness. We say the universe, God, is conscious. The universe isn't random, because if it were, scientists wouldn't be able to, for example, do any of their calculations. It's only because of natural laws and known patterns that we are able to navigate the world. You can infer the intelligence behind all creation. Everything here is just knowledge made manifest. How else do you get a towering oak from a small acorn? For this reason, we say the universe is conscious and intelligent."

"You mean 'intelligent design'?" the atheist added with a smirk.

"Right, it's one area where we're in agreement with the Bible thumpers. Anyway, so up until now we've learned that God is a figurative entity — a name for consciousness or awareness, plus various powers including the knowledge, energy and matter to make stuff. We'll call these powers *maya*. From this we're able to state:

Awareness + maya = God.

"Okay, so we've defined God. But what about a person?

Awareness + a body-mind = a person.

"Interestingly enough, both God and a person have awareness. Follow? Everything just resolves back into awareness, even God and God's stuff. It's a bit counterintuitive, but the essence of the universe isn't dark matter or even energy. It's pure, attributeless, non-dual awareness. With me so far?"

"I think so... So, you're proposing we are the same as God?"

"Yes and no," replied the sage. "We share the same essence as God—just like all clay pots are made of clay—but obviously we cannot wield God's powers and we aren't omniscient or omnipresent. We are God from the perspective that we are a product of God and by the fact that we share the same essence— awareness—but that's as far as it goes. But let's not diminish the fact that we share the same source—that's pretty cool. It also helps to remind us that everything has been given to us, including this body, mind and intellect. But back to your question, 'What created God?' Where it gets tricky is when we look at all of God's stuff. We say God's creation is beginningless. God's creation is beginningless because it exists in awareness and awareness, we like to say, is a causeless cause. Awareness just is. It's what is never born and never dies. Awareness has no limitations because if it did, it wouldn't be whole, complete, changeless, or non-dual. We say awareness is real and all objects, including thoughts, are only apparently real." The sage paused a moment before clarifying, "By the way, 'real' is defined as that which is always present and never changes. Objects — and that includes thoughts and emotions too — are always changing and unreliable, so they don't qualify. All objects are also made up of other objects, unlike awareness, which is whole, complete, and not dependent on other objects. Now this is the tricky part: Because all objects are only apparently real — meaning, they are always changing into something else — they are beginningless, because something that isn't real can never be born. Are you still with me?"

"You're making my head explode! Objects don't exist now?" exclaimed the atheist with disbelief.

"Objects do exist because they are experienced, but they are not real. They are *apparently* real. It's just like the story of the guy who mistakes a coiled rope for a snake. At first, the rope is a snake. It's not until the truth is known that the 'snake' becomes a rope again. The 'snake' is experienced but isn't real. Objects exist because we experience them, but on closer examination they flunk the test. They are ephemeral, passing—something one moment and something else, the next."

"So, then what are objects?"

"When looked at closely, objects are just a temporary aggregate of smaller parts, but really they are just thoughts. All objects exist as thoughts. We don't actually sense objects, just their properties — color, shape, texture, taste, and smell. From the various sensory inputs, the mind automatically takes the properties, puts them together and applies a name and form, so that, for example, *wet* and *translucent* becomes 'water' and *yellow*, *hot*, and *crackling* becomes 'fire.'"

"So, we're living in a thought universe?"

"Bingo! How's that for non-dual vision!"

"Um... Okay, I guess. But you still haven't answered my

question."

"Right, 'Where does God come from?' Let's see... Because awareness is never born and never dies, awareness is eternal. And because awareness is eternal, so is God. Remember, the essence of God is just awareness and because awareness is beginningless and God's stuff exists within awareness, God is beginningless. Since God has no beginning, God is not born. God simply is. So, the question is moot. But here's the catch— God isn't real either."

"Wait... What?" replied the atheist, now visually annoyed. "You just took 15 minutes to argue your case for God and now you're telling me God isn't real? I guess that proves my point."

"Which is?"

"There is no God."

"Remember what I said: by our definition only awareness is real. God only exists because of awareness. God is dependent on awareness and so, is only apparently real, just like all God's stuff. Nevertheless, we still experience God's creation. So, you can't just write-off God. You're in this dreamscape whether you like it or not! Everything you have is given to you, even if it isn't real by our definition. God isn't to be dismissed; God is to be known!"

"But how is God able to create anything and most importantly, why would it want to?" asked the atheist.

"I don't know, maybe God was bored? Or maybe God just wanted to know itself so it created conscious beings with sense organs in order to see, smell, taste, touch and hear its creation? It's a mystery why anything exists at all! The deeper you dive into this creation, the more bizarre it gets. Open one door and there's another, and another — an endless succession of doors to be opened. Or you can look at it like a puzzle folded within another puzzle, where the macrocosmic mirrors the microcosmic and vice versa. It's seeing the ocean in a drop of water and all that."

"How so?"

"God's stuff is just patterns, patterns everywhere... and God is very frugal! Take nature's fractals, for example. The veins under your skin appear as the veins in a leaf, which look like the branches of a tree, which appear the same as lightning in the sky, and so on and so on... Nature is just a fixed set of laws with the same patterns applied over and over again. From a few we get the many, just like from the 26 letters of the alphabet we're able to assemble thousands of words, essays and cheap romance novels. So what do you think of God so far?"

"To me, it sounds like you're just explaining nature but in a way that suggests there is an awareness and intelligence behind it."

"Yep, God isn't about guilt, fear or asking for the latest gaming console. God is to be worshiped, not because we should fear God, but because we know we aren't in control."

"Control of what?"

"*This*, the results. Once you know God and how God's field of experience works, you just let go. You really have no choice. It's complete acceptance and with that, a big sigh of relief, frankly."

"But I have free will, I don't need to negotiate with God."

"Even if you could, God's laws are non-negotiable and from your point of view, you do have free will and a certain degree of control. But looking at the big picture, you're totally dependent on God. It should be obvious that there's a network of constant support operating here. Americans, in particular, take pride in self-reliance, but it's all just an illusion—something writers romanticizing about the Old West made up. You didn't do anything to get to where you're at. Why, you couldn't even..."

"Just wait a minute, I..."

"Look," interrupted the sage sensing things were getting a bit hot, "everything has been given to you — your parents, your home, your education, your clothing, your food, your partner, your recreation... Don't you see the infinite actions that had to take place so that you could be here talking to me right now?" the sage asked emphatically. "There's an old Zen monk who likes to say he can see the whole universe in a single sheet of paper... and he's right! Look at everything that had to occur for even a single sheet of paper to manifest — the sun, the water, the tree, the lumberjack, the chainsaw, the truck, the sawmill, the paper factory, the retailer, the salesperson... The sheet of paper didn't just manifest itself and neither did you or any of that which you believe you have control of. Your sense of control is just an illusion. All results come from the field. Do you see how this works? *No action takes place without the blessing of all things in the field.* Not even your ability to make decisions." The sage then added, "How much control do you have even over your own thoughts?"

"Um... Okay," replied the atheist searching for a comeback. "But if your God exists and is so wonderful then why all the evil and bloodshed in the world? Why would anyone worship such a masochist?"   •

"God doesn't cause the world's problems; ignorance of God does. People act out of desire and fear and create suffering. Take away ignorance and everything is totally fine with the universe, even death. Furthermore, in this world of duality nothing exists without its opposite. You cannot have hot without cold, sweet without sour, or beautiful without the mundane. What would you have 'beautiful' to compare with if everything were beautiful?"

"You have an answer for everything, don't you? How do I know this isn't just another elaborate story made up by some old guy living in a cave?"

"Hey, this isn't a smart-a-thon to see who can make the other guy paint himself into a corner. There are no winners. We're all swimming in the same fish bowl here. I'm just calling out what you and everyone else already intuitively know. We might not be able to put our finger on it, so we come up with all kinds of names for it — Krishna, Allah, Jehovah, 'Him,' 'Her'… whatever you want to call it—it doesn't really matter. It's all impersonal, like the weather. But you might find there's a certain usefulness to having God-knowledge. It helps alleviate ignorance — the cause of suffering — and it promotes good habits like gratitude and letting go — two of the best remedies for stress. You and I can argue all day and night whether or not God exists. But one thing you cannot deny is *this*, that is, this experience. You cannot deny that what you're witnessing is being simultaneously created, maintained, and recycled by a power greater than you. This you cannot deny, my friend. Call it nature if you will, I'll stick with God."

Introduction

Let's face it, "God" is an awkward topic for most westerners. God is rarely spoken of outside a house of worship and rarely, among friends or even family. As a society we are more comfortable discussing our sex life than we are God. On the rare occasion the G-word does slip out, our knee-jerk reaction is to shuffle, duck and dodge. In short, God is now a private affair best kept to oneself in fear of offending the neighbors.

But God's unpopularity doesn't end there. According to a Gallup poll,[1] in 2020 just 47% of US adults belonged to a church, synagogue or mosque. This was the first time in the history of the poll that membership had dropped below 50%—which is remarkable considering that just twenty-two years earlier the number of US adults affiliated with a church, synagogue or mosque was almost 75%.

Growing up Catholic in the '70s and '80s, I was taught that God was to be respected, even feared. Pressured by my parents to attend catechism, I was fed God and Jesus stories in hopes that they would somehow, through osmosis, instill some virtue in me. Looking back, I remember very little of my catechism due to a lack of interest in what can only be described as a seething anger for being force-fed religious doctrine. Even back then, I had no interest in joining the flock.

It was my mother's idea that I should go to catechism and my scientist father's understanding that if I didn't, we would both be in the dog house. Mom was a strict practicing Catholic who had been educated by nuns in a small midwestern, Canadian town. Unfortunately, the nuns had instilled in her at a young age a strong sense of guilt. Once married and advised by a priest against using any birth control, my parents had four children—which was more than they could handle given their second having special needs. Nevertheless, in spite of the constant tension at home, we somehow always made it to mass on Sundays. Afterwards, we would reward ourselves for withstanding exactly sixty minutes of mind-numbing vapidity with the sugar-high, pure bliss of glazed donuts. God, indeed, was good!

One of the few memories I have of those catechism days is that of a self-righteous old traditionalist with black hairs growing out of her chin. She made it a point to teach us boys that we were all committing a great sin if we ever looked at a girlie magazine—which, as you probably guessed, only made the possibility of doing so that more intriguing. The majority of the catechism teachers were gentle souls just looking for a spiritual outlet and a meaningful way to give their time to the community, but this one was from another era—the era in which my mother grew up; a time when fear was the preferred teaching method for establishing a special closeness to God and making certain mischievous boys and girls stay in line. It was a militant approach used more for disciplinary reasons than spiritual ones—as it has been for centuries by tyrants and old catechism teachers alike.

Nevertheless, in spite of never fulfilling my mother's wish that I embrace Catholicism, it was hard to write off God who, throughout my youth, always remained a kind of lingering curiosity; a superstition; a super-stalker watching my every move. God was the perpetual nagging parental-figure-in-the-sky making judgment and calling out my every weakness and moral slip-up. However, God was also who I turned to when I needed a little help. He was a last resort; a lottery ticket in hopes of gaining whatever it was that was currently out of reach: a new guitar, a surfboard, a cool car... a girlfriend I could be proud of.

As I grew up and entered my twenties, God was mitigated to the background and even more so when it became obvious that his long resume of awesome credentials and affiliations began to include such events as the Bosnian war (fought mostly along ethno-religious lines), the hypocrisy of Catholic priests (several having sexually abused young boys), and of course, the lunacy of Islamic extremists flying into skyscrapers (in order to, supposedly, restore God's rule and destroy the infidels).

Later, married, and in my thirties with a little life experience under my belt, I had already concluded that faith in God didn't add up. I began to disdain God and religion in general and openly expressed my newly found atheism. I was convinced that God was just a belief from a bygone age of bloodthirsty men, steel, and plague; that God was a fantasy, an imaginary friend; a security blanket for childlike minds awaiting a better afterlife. Historically speaking, I saw God as the curmudgeon from the Old Testament who commanded the slaughter of the Canaanites, and "He" who was the "soul-cleansing" inspiration behind the Crusades. Even today, I still see God used as an absurd justification for ethnic-cleansing, political oppression and the run-away consumption of the earth's (remaining) animals, plants and resources.[2]

Questions began to arise: "Why God?" "Where is God?" "If God created the world, then who created God?" Arguments emerged at the family table. Mom was now having to defend her faith. As for me, I had already decided there was no room for God in my life.

God was out!

But the religious impulse is strong and as hardwired in us as the desire to know our own true identity. For many, even "non-believers," the fear of sudden misfortune and the inevitability of death keeps the flame going. Furthermore, a life without seeking to understand the spirit is a life that feels empty and incomplete. After all, there's got to be more to it than just chasing every pleasure and avoiding every fear. For those of us inclined to look within, we may refuse the tradition of our parents but seek an alternative means to getting in touch with the spirit. Given adequate time, curiosity and the means to explore the landscape, many signs point east.

For me, what began as a wish to develop a sense of calm and find refuge from the insane corporate environment of the early dot-com years, turned into a genuine interest in mind-management and a desire to understand my experience. The hippies' early adventures had already cut a clear path to Buddhism, Taoism and Yoga. "Why not look there?" I thought. I didn't even need to get on a plane and travel to some exotic part of the world in order to live on whatever I had in my pocket, all the while meditating in some snake infested forest.

I grew up in California, the Bay Area—a cultural mélange if there ever was one—which meant eastern spirituality was already accessible in the form of meditation centers that occupied old repurposed steeple churches and in residential retreat centers tucked away in the beautiful Carmel Valley and Marin countryside; not to mention the dozens of books popping · up like lotus flowers in bookstores everywhere. With our first child on the way, as well as the burden of becoming a parent, I now persisted in learning everything I could about spirituality, reading countless books and waking up early to spend the early hours in silent meditation.

It wasn't until several years later at the end of a long journey that spanned Pre-Socratic philosophy, Stoicism, American Transcendentalism, the comparative studies of Joseph Campbell, the mindfulness practice of Vipassana Buddhism, and the Self-inquiry of Advaita, that I realized the value of God.

But this isn't a book about being "born again," nor is it some prodigal son parable. Rediscovering God was never in my plans because I could never imagine a God any different from the one I was brought up to believe in. Even today, my friends and family are surprised by my newly gained interest in what I had once conclusively decided wasn't a topic worth talking about.

It's a bit ironic that my eventual reacquaintance with

God came from the East. Most westerners associate Eastern spirituality with yoga, meditation and "being one with the universe." Most probably aren't even aware that the widely known Bhagavad Gita translated from Sanskrit means "The Song of God." And even though God as "Ishvara" is mentioned in traditional Indo-Aryan texts, such as Patanjali's *Yoga Sutras*, it's seldom mentioned by western teachers who teach their own brand of yoga, or by those who like to cherry-pick ideas from the Upanishads in order to put their own personal spin on non-duality. This is probably a surprise to no one. After all, western seekers want enlightenment,[3] not God.

It was through my eventual discovery and teachings of traditional Advaita Vedanta— an ancient method for examining our experience—that I learned that the concept of God had a certain value and utility. What had suddenly peaked my interest in God wasn't an impassioned devotion to a supreme entity or the intoxicating elixir of universal love but rather, God as a means for understanding the world and my place in it.

Through Vedanta I learned that to know God is to feel comfortable with what is—that is, with this apparent world, person and that which is witness to it all (more about that later). I also learned that to know God is to understand what the sages talk about when they say the world is perfect as it is and can't be any different. And I learned that to truly know God is to have the satisfaction of knowing that whatever happens, I'm okay.

I also began to understand that faith in God should be approached like a walking stick we use until the time arrives that we're able to walk on our own two feet (such is the proper definition and use of religion). Faith should be where you start your journey, not where you finish it. What so few ever realize is that there is such a thing as having God-knowledge and that one needn't be satisfied with mere beliefs and illogical answers to life's biggest questions. In fact, the answers have always been there just waiting to be uncovered (such is the nature of the truth—and of God).

Lastly, I learned that God is important because without God, what should one do with the ego which always seems to get in the way of spiritual progress? The ego's ability to persuade us into believing we are separate, unique individuals apart from the rest of creation is so preposterous and yet, so persistent that without having an understanding of God we are left powerless to its many whims. Knowledge of God reminds us that we aren't detached from creation, that we aren't really in control, and that in spite of a consumer society that encourages ownership of everything, we are in actuality, owners of nothing.

Thus, the cognitive shift I had after my journey wasn't derived from belief but from understanding. In the past, I always struggled with believing in God, but now I could *know* God. The difference is night and day for the seeker. The problem with believing in God is that if I believe in God, I'm making a judgment before ever knowing. I'm saying God may or may not exist. With belief, there is always a sense of uncertainty and reliance on non-verifiable facts that as a thinking person, I'm not comfortable with. Furthermore, if I can only believe in God and not know God, how am I expected to interact with God, let alone have any real relationship with God? If God is only a belief for me, I'm at risk of asking the wrong questions or worse, being disappointed when my expectations of God aren't met.

Once you have God-knowledge, questions such as "Where does God live?" "What does God look like?" "Will I ever meet God?" seem childish. They reflect a certain naiveté just as they would if the same questions were asked about any universal power, for example, gravity. You would probably never ask, "Where is gravity?" "What does gravity look like?" "How can I meet this gravity?" Simply put, so many of us never find the answers to questions about God because we are asking the wrong questions! For starters, our first question shouldn't be "Where is God?" or "How can I see God?" but instead, "*What* is God?" Because without first defining God, we run the risk of pursuing something totally different, or something that logically doesn't even make sense.

How we define God matters just as much, if not more, than what we believe or understand about God. For example, let's say I ask you about some random word. Let's say the word is "cherimoya." You respond with a flummoxed look, so to keep you guessing I tell you it's a physical object—which somewhat narrows the scope but still leaves you with too many options. Next, I tell you it's a fruit, and all of a sudden, you're able to come up with dozens of related questions: "What shape is it?" "What color is it?" "Where is it grown?" "What does it taste like?" "How many seeds does it have?" etc. So, until we know the *what*, we can't even know if *why* or a *where* are applicable.

So, then... What is God?

Simply put, God is everything that exists including existence itself. But more to the point, God is both the consciousness and creative principles, which are referred to in the book as God 1 and God 2. The first is the formless "spirit," while the other is the matter and intelligence that make up the material world. Throughout the book, I'll approach God using logic, inference and good old common sense. I will also take inspiration from the Bhagavad Gita, the Upanishads and other texts in order to show God's two-fold nature.

As an aside, in many ways this book is a follow-up to an earlier book of mine, *The Teachings of the Bhagavad Gita*, where, with the aid of various Advaita Vedanta masters, I was able to unlock the meaning of the Gita. This book takes that knowledge and attempts to describe it in more detail using additional sources, while also introducing new perspectives, such as God as one great order (Chapter 4), God and the question of free will (part of Chapter 5), and whether or not God is love (Chapter 7). I have also included a section in the addendum that answers questions that were not specifically covered in the book's chapters.

Lastly, the objective of this book isn't to help the reader become a God-believer but instead, a God-knower. God has become unpopular these days because for many of us, God simply doesn't make sense anymore. It's my hope that this book in some small way helps one to reconsider God—not as another veiled attempt to making you feel guilty about being an imperfect human being (I promise, it won't do that), but to better understand our experience and place in the cosmos.

Notes

1. Jones, Jeffrey M. "U.S. Church Membership Falls Below Majority for First time." *Gallup.* https://news.gallup.com/poll/341963/church-membership-falls-below-majority-first-time.aspx
2. "And God blessed them, and God said unto them, Be fruitful, and multiply, and replenish the earth, and subdue it: and have dominion over the fish of the sea, and over the fowl of the air, and over every living thing that moveth upon the earth" (Genesis 1.28).
3. In spite of the popular belief that enlightenment is an achievable supernatural reality, in actuality it's a mythological concept mostly based on a misunderstanding of the ancient texts, magical thinking and the hope that by finding the right spiritual practice life will become, literally, a walk in the clouds. In contrast, Vedanta suggests that enlightenment (a.k.a., *moksha* or spiritual liberation) is not gained through any kind of mystical experience or special event. From Vedanta's cut-and-dried perspective, enlightenment is simply the removal of ignorance.

Chapter 1

God 1

We begin with God 1, the consciousness principle or the higher of God's two-fold nature, not because God 1 is the easiest of the two to understand (it's not), but because it's the ground of all experience and that which comes before everything else. As ordinary consciousness/awareness,[1] God 1 seems easy to define and yet, it's the most difficult of the two to realize. What makes God 1 so difficult is that it never falls into our actual line of site, and that's because it is formless, actionless, and has no attributes and therefore, is not an object available to our senses. The concealed nature of God 1 is often compared in the Upanishads[2] to the oil hidden in oil-seed, the butter hidden in milk or the fire hidden in wood. The point is that it takes an inquisitive mind to see that which isn't made manifest.

At our most fundamental level, God 1 is the non-experiencing "witness" that each of us carries within us (and even that is saying too much). In fact, because it is not an object, the most accurate way to describe God 1 is by stating what it's not—which is essentially everything, including not the body, not the mind, not the intellect, not the ego, and paradoxically, not non-existence either.

In the Mandukya Upanishad, it's written that God 1:

> is not that which is conscious of the subjective inner world, nor that which is conscious of the objective outer world, nor that which is conscious of both, nor that which is a mass of consciousness. It is not simple consciousness nor is it unconsciousness. It is unperceived, unrelated, incomprehensible, uninferable, unthinkable, and indescribable. (7)

For most of us, such verses don't leave us much the wiser. So, Vedanta—an ancient wisdom tradition which is derived from the Upanishads—often begins with words and phrases such as "formless," "immutable," "eternal," "self-luminous," "all-pervading" and "subtler than the subtle," to suggest the nature of God 1. And while all words ultimately fall short in describing the indescribable, when applied skillfully, they can help to gently guide the inquirer toward an understanding.

God 1 is a radical teaching because it requires a cognitive shift to seeing who, or more accurately, *what* you are. Not only is God 1 hard to understand due to our inability to perceive it (including with any and all scientific instruments), but because our ignorance is hardwired and knowledge of God 1 is difficult to grasp. For this reason, it's traditionally taught only to those who have the following: (1) discrimination—the ability to tell the difference between what's true and what's not (2) dispassion—a lack of interest in worldly objects due to the results of discrimination (3) discipline—management of the mind and senses, as well as (4) a burning desire to know the truth. This isn't to say that only a chosen few can ever know God 1, but rather, that the mind needs to be prepared and made steady in order to see that which is not apparent. To "see" in this case isn't to suggest having some kind of chance mystical experience, but rather, to be able to look beyond that which obscures the truth. For example, a mind that is constantly agitated with desire or fear, or a mind that is numb or clouded, is probably not ready to hear such a teaching.

God 1 is the essence of what you are, which should, one would assume, make it easy to identify. If we ask a pot to show its essence, it will remind us it's clay. If we ask a wave, it will remind us it's water. In both cases, the pot and the wave are just name and form shaped out of something else.

As individuals, we know we are conscious because it is self-evident. Our parents never had to teach us the concept "I am." However, where doubt arises is with the nature of "I." We might ask, "Is this 'I am' experienced as the body?" Is it the mind? Is it matter or spirit, or maybe something else we haven't yet considered?"

As mysterious as it seems (one for which science struggles to understand), consciousness is actually impersonal, ordinary, and pervasive on our little planet and most likely throughout the universe. What's not ordinary is the understanding that the consciousness in you, is the same consciousness in me, which is the same consciousness that is behind all creation. Vedanta suggests that all of creation comes out of consciousness and that our error is, simply, that we are unable to see the cause in the effect. For example, when we look at a pot, we might fail to notice that it is just clay, or when we look at a wave, we might fail to notice that it's just water. Likewise, when we look at any object, we fail to see that ultimately, it's just consciousness in the form of a thought. We become so fixed on the effect that we forget to stop and ask what it is we're actually observing. We are like the proverbial fish never stopping to notice water.

According to Vedanta, consciousness is the ground of all being—the "one without a second." Thus, if God 1 is non-dual consciousness—meaning everything comes out of it—and the same consciousness that exists in you exists in me, then we are already connected to God and just don't know it! It's this understanding and union with God that is the highest realization. It's also the main theme of the Bhagavad Gita.

In the Gita, we are given a full view into God's nature. Krishna, as God incarnate, first reveals his true identity to his friend, the warrior-prince Arjuna, when he says:

There never was a time I did not exist, nor you, nor these kings. And there will never be a time any of us ceases to exist. (2.12)

Krishna is letting Arjuna in on a little secret. The knowledge of God 1 is a secret because ignorance is hardwired and even once the knowledge is taught, only a few will understand it. The knowledge is also a secret because it's counterintuitive and is difficult to learn without a guide. If I want to know my physical appearance, I need a mirror, but if I want to know God—I need another kind of mirror.

The Means of Knowledge

To understand how we can know God 1 as consciousness we must first examine how, as individuals, we acquire knowledge. Vedanta outlines five means of knowledge. The first is **direct perception**. This is knowledge obtained through the immediate contact of objects as they are interpreted by the senses. If someone asks how is it that you know such-and-such object, you might answer because you saw it, smelled it, touched it, heard it or tasted it.

The second means of knowledge is **non-perception**. This is a means of knowing through a negative fact gained through the absence of a particular thing. For example, I know it didn't rain last night because it isn't wet outside, or I know my daughter didn't eat her dinner because it is still on the table.

The third is **inference**, which is indirect knowledge. Inference is something that leads to direct knowledge. The classic example is where there's smoke there must be fire. In this case, the perceived (smoke) has an invariable connection with the non-perceived (fire). Thus, knowledge of one leads to knowledge of another.

The fourth means of knowledge is **postulation**, another indirect means of knowledge. This is the knowledge obtained when the known fact cannot be accounted for without the existence of another fact which is not known. For example, my daughter says she goes to bed at 9 p.m. every school night. Sunday through Thursday she is observed going to her bedroom and turning off her light at exactly 9 p.m. However, everyday her alarm goes off at 7 a.m. and she refuses to get out of bed. Recently it was discovered that she sleeps with her phone. Taking the phone into account, it's clear that she is staying up late on her phone and therefore, not getting enough sleep. So, the fourth means is knowledge through deduction.

Lastly, the fifth means of knowledge, and the third indirect means, is **comparison**. This is obtaining knowledge of an unknown object by comparing it with another known object. For instance, in order for you to know what a parsnip tastes like, I might liken it to another root vegetable you're familiar with—a carrot. So, by comparison with something that is already known, there is a transfer of knowledge.

Of the five means of knowledge, direct perception and non-perception have perception as their base, while inference, postulation and comparison have inference as theirs. So to summarize, knowledge can be gained either through perception or inference.

However, to know God 1 none of these means of knowledge will suffice. The sense instruments and the mind through which the senses function only work when given a sense object to be aware of. God 1 is not an object, so perception and inference are ineffectual. So, until I find both a proper means of knowledge to understanding God 1 and a guide who has the ability to unfold the knowledge, I can't know what it is I don't know! This is why knowing God 1 is so tricky, because God 1 is not discoverable using any of the normal means of knowledge.

Vedanta is sometimes compared with a mirror, because it shows or reflects that which cannot be known by any other means. Thus, scripture, which reveals the knowledge of God 1, is counted as a sixth means of knowledge. Its purpose is to negate all the positive attributes falsely associated with absolute reality. Just like to understand that matter is energy you need physics, to understand consciousness as the essence of all existence, you need scripture. Scriptural knowledge must then be followed by reflection or removing doubt. Reflection amounts to the individual testing the validity of what he or she has learned through a qualified teacher. Faith is also a qualification for arriving at the truth, but it's always faith pending one's own investigation. In the end, the means of knowledge leading to the truth must not leave any uncertainty.

The Subject and the Object

Let's start with a simple observation: If God 1 is not any object, it must be the subject—and it is! God 1 is the only true subject. The Brihadaranyaka Upanishad recognizes the difficulty of knowing God 1 as the ultimate subject when it states:

> You cannot see that which is the witness of vision. You cannot hear that which is the hearer of hearing. You cannot think of that which is the thinker of thought. You cannot know that which is the knower of knowledge... (3.4.2)

So the first thing to know about God 1 is that you're never going to find it because you are it! Just like fire which cannot burn or illumine itself, we cannot know that which is "the knower of knowledge" because we are that which we seek to know. That which we cannot know can't be the senses or the mind because it's what comes before the senses and the mind. For example, the eye may be thought of as the perceiver of the changing phenomena of the outer world, the mind as the perceiver of the changing conditions of the organ of vision, and consciousness as the perceiver of the changing states of the mind. However, nothing precedes consciousness or is the perceiver of consciousness because consciousness is the unchanging substrate: the fundamental perceiver of all experience.

As the subject, all objects rise and subside within consciousness. For example, both the body and the mind are only accessible to me in the waking state and not in the dream or deep sleep states. This shows that the body and mind can't be me because (1) they are objects known to me—the subject—and (2) because they aren't always present. The only reason we identify with the body and the mind is because of their proximity and staying power.

The body-mind is sometimes compared with a red-hot iron, and consciousness, its burning effect. The burning comes from the fire within the iron and is not intrinsic to the iron. The iron doesn't burn, the fire does. Similarly, when consciousness is brought into contact with an object via the senses, the senses are not what is aware of the object, consciousness is. The senses are just data-collecting instruments.

Neither does the mind make any contact with an object because it too, is non-luminous. Its power to think is derived from the light of consciousness shining within, which pervades all its various states. So, pure consciousness (meaning, consciousness without any attributes) is the ultimate subject. Even in deep sleep, consciousness is still there as the witness of the non-activity of the mind. If that weren't the case, sleep would equate to death.

Vedanta teaches that the mind is an inert and insentient material entity with a reflective-like quality. It needs consciousness in order to apprehend an object because it is not the mind but the "light" of consciousness reflected in the mind that makes awareness of an object possible. Thus, experience occurs only when there is consciousness plus a mind. It's for this reason, when we are in deep sleep, we aren't conscious of anything because the mind is not there to experience any objects.

This practice of discriminating objects from the subject is important for overcoming our deep-rooted misidentification. Only through sustained inquiry can we change the hardwired notion that we are the body-mind and redirect it toward our true identity—universal consciousness (God 1). One way to develop discrimination is through such practices as mindfulness meditation, which is a way to observe the objects of the mind (thoughts) on the screen of consciousness without interacting with them or trying to change them in any way. While sitting in silent meditation, we can observe that the mind actually has a mind of its own and recognize there's a gap between the knower and the known; the subject and the object.

God 1 as Brahman

God 1 is often referred to in Vedic scripture as "Brahman." Brahman (not to be confused with "Brahma," the Hindu mythological creator of the universe, or with "Brahmin," the Hindu priestly class) is representative of absolute reality and the indivisible ground of all being. Brahman in Sanskrit means "bigger than the biggest" or that which accommodates everything. Brahman is not an actual entity but instead synonymous with pure consciousness. If space is that which accommodates all objects, Brahman is that which accommodates all objects plus space (space being just another object known by consciousness). So, Brahman encompasses space, time, matter, as well as all subtle objects, even thoughts. There is nothing Brahman doesn't encompass.

As the absolute, Brahman is indivisible. Otherwise, there would be no end to the universe dividing into ever-smaller parts, nor any common substrate to support the experience of such an endless division (which would be illogical). Thus, the division of objects into ever-increasing diminutive parts eventually leads not to no-thing, but to Brahman. Take away all of creation and what you have left is Brahman. Brahman is that which cannot be divided, modified, removed or negated.

As another name for God 1, Brahman will be useful in Chapter 3 when we discuss how out of formless consciousness, Vedanta proposes we get the world.

Existence-Consciousness-Bliss

The three traditional epithets for Brahman are existence, consciousness and bliss. These are not separate attributes of Brahman but instead, synonyms, such that we say Brahman is existence-consciousness-bliss, or in Sanskrit, *sat-chit-ananda*. Brahman as consciousness has already been explained as the substrate to all that we experience. In this way, consciousness pervades all objects. But what does it mean to define Brahman as existence?

Existence is pure being. Existence is the "I am" when I say "*I am* a man," "*I am* a father," *I am* a son," etc. In truth, I cannot be anything other than "I am" because, as we'll soon learn, only "I am" constitutes absolute reality. As individuals, nobody must tell us we are conscious because it is already obvious that "I am." Take away everything you identify with — including the body, mind and senses — and "I am" is what remains. Brahman, as being, always exists without a past or future because it is that which is outside of time and space. The "I am" when you are one year old is the same "I am" when you are one hundred.

The is-ness of our everyday contact with objects is also existence. For example, it's an illusion that existence of an object belongs to the object. When we see a mountain, we say the mountain exists. But the mountain doesn't exist as something the mountain does. Instead, we should say "existence mountains" because existence is the subject for every object, not the object itself. Thus, existence pervades all objects. The nature of existence is six-fold: (1) existence is not a part, product or property of the object (2) existence is not limited by the boundaries of objects (3) existence survives even without objects (4) existence is only experienced in association with an object (5) existence has no divisions and (6) existence alone is pure consciousness.

Lastly, "bliss" is often misinterpreted in the spiritual world to be an experiential state of joy and something to strive for through action. The word "bliss" may elicit images of enlightened souls meditating on swirling clouds, indifferent to the world below. However, instead of defining bliss as happiness, in this case it's more accurate to define it as *the perfect satisfaction as a result of the absence of any limitation*. In fact, "limitlessness" is sometimes used instead of "bliss" in order to remove the confusion with Brahman being some kind of state of ecstasy (Brahman is not a state or a feeling). So, when Brahman is described as bliss, it's really showing that its nature is absolute freedom. All objects are of the nature to bind, only formless Brahman is of the nature to be limitless.

Defining What Is Real

In the verse from the Bhagavad Gita below, Krishna emphasizes that which differentiates God 1 from everything else:

> There is no being for that which is unreal, there is no non-being for that which is real. This is known by the seers of the truth. That which pervades the entire world cannot be destroyed, for there can be no destruction for that which is always present and never changes. (2.16–17)

This distinction between that which is real and that which isn't is critical to understanding God 1. God 1 co-exists with everything but in a different order of reality, which allows it to remain pure and uncorrupted. This separation is often compared to a movie screen that in spite of the drama and destruction projected on it, is left untouched.

In Sanskrit, there are many ways to describe the absolute that allows an individual to approach God from different angles and understanding. One term that is often used is *satya*, meaning, that which is true or real. In contrast, *mithya* is that which is illusory or "apparently" real. Mithya includes all objects in the universe. Objects appear real but on closer examination are found to be dependent, impermanent and made of smaller parts. Objects are also constantly changing and are not always present.

In Gaudapada's *The Mandukya Upanishad with Karika* it's stated:

> That which doesn't exist in the beginning nor in the end is the same in the present. Objects are like illusions and yet, they are regarded as real. (2.6)

So, when Vedanta says objects are not real, it's not saying they don't exist like a square circle doesn't exist, but that like a mirage they don't have any actual substance. From our limited perspective, most objects appear concrete and stable. But if we were able to speed up time — like one of those time-lapse videos which shows a beautiful bowl of fruit slowly decomposing over a span of days and weeks — we would recognize that in fact, all objects are constantly in the process of becoming something else. Furthermore, all objects are dependent on other objects. For example, a shirt is made of fabric, which is made of thread, which is made of cotton, which is made up of cellulose fiber, and so on. So, really, a form is just a form of a form of a form, etc.

Because all of nature is divisible, it makes it difficult to say where an object actually starts and where it ends. Even something as subtle as air is still an object made up of other objects (nitrogen, oxygen, carbon dioxide, etc.). In fact, we are only really able to define an object by the composition of its parts. If we take a car and remove its wheels, is it still a car? What if we remove the engine? What if we remove everything and just leave the steering wheel? We might ask, at what point did it stop becoming a car? For this reason the wise say the world is like a dream, because everything is constantly changing and nothing ever is what it seems.

It goes without mention that all objects are divisible right down to the atomic level (which, as it turns out, is mostly empty space). But it doesn't stop there. If we examine our actual experience of objects we might come to the startling realization that all objects are really just thoughts.

As the sage in the dialogue with the atheist explains:

We don't actually sense objects, just their properties — color, shape, texture, taste, smell, etc. From the various sensory inputs, the mind automatically takes the properties, puts them together and applies a name and form, so that, for example, *wet* and *translucent* becomes "water" and *yellow, hot,* and *crackling* becomes "fire."

From this we can conclude that there is no "there" there and that our universe is actually a thought universe!

On the other hand, that which is satya never changes, is always present and is not divisible. Satya was there before the world and will be there afterwards. It was never not. Satya, of course, is synonymous with consciousness. Thus, we already have many different names for God 1.

For the inquirer, the goal is to then take the knowledge of satya/mithya and constantly discriminate between what is real and what isn't. The benefit is that once we identify with that which is real (satya), we can stand on solid ground instead of the shifting sands of time (mithya). In contrast, identifying with this aging, disease-prone, slowly disintegrating body, only brings about suffering. Thus, this body-mind is mithya but the truth of what I am is satya—pure, ordinary, partless, everlasting, limitless, non-dual consciousness.

An understanding of mithya and satya will be useful throughout the rest of the book as we continue to discriminate between what's real and what's not.

The Self

God 1 is not only pure consciousness, but the consciousness that all beings apparently embody. This embodiment of God 1 represents our true self. To make the distinction between God 1 (original consciousness) and God 1 as embodied consciousness (borrowed consciousness), we'll call God 1-embodied the "Self" with a capital "S" to distinguish it from the small imaginary self (the ego). This also helps recognize that while God 1 and I are one, I am not God in the sense that I am the all-knowing creator of the universe (God 2).

The embodiment of God 1 in all beings makes the one appear to be the many and varied. To give an example of how the embodiment of the Self works, you might imagine each of us like a bucket of water lined up in the sun reflecting the one, same light. There are buckets of different sizes, colors and shape, but regardless of the kind of bucket, each reflects the same light.

Another example is how air that is blown through a musical instrument will sound different depending on whether the instrument is a flute, oboe or saxophone. There are of course many different kinds of wind instruments, but they all seemingly come to life when a musician blows air through one end of it.

In summary, God 1 is what unites all of us in spite of our seeming differences. This commonality between us is subtle and yet, so obvious that it's totally missed. Once the Self is realized, it's hard not to feel a connection to all beings — including plants, animals and the entire biosphere — because my light/your light/ all living beings' light is from the same source. Not only are we of the same formless essence, but our physical bodies are made up of the same basic gross and subtle elements, which means upon close examination, any apparent variations between us are negligible — like two waves claiming to be different from each other.

To see the difference between Brahman and the Self, think of Brahman as the absolute reality behind the universe and the Self as the absolute reality behind the individual. The final objective, then, is to see that both are actually one and the same. In other words, both Brahman and the Self are God 1.

A common invocation at the beginning of the Upanishads states:

> That is full, this is full. This fullness has been projected from that fullness. When this fullness merges in that fullness, all that remains is fullness.

Fullness, wholeness, completeness... these are words often used to describe the nature of the Self because when I am perfectly aligned with the Self, I no longer need to seek objects in an effort to make myself feel complete. The hunger within subsides and in its place, there is bliss—pure satisfaction.

With the realization that God 1 is me as the embodied Self, I am able to shift my identity and recognize that:[3]

I am whole, complete, non-dual, actionless, unlimited, unchanging, ever-present, ordinary consciousness.

I am already that which I seek. It was there all along and I just wasn't able to see it. It is also stated here that I (consciousness) am "actionless" because I am not the doer. My presence as consciousness is that which makes the doer and the doing possible. I am simply the still, blank screen upon which the doer and the objects of experience are projected.

I am the source of all happiness and joy because I need nothing to complete me.

Duality (the world of objects and the belief they are real) is by its nature, limiting. Non-duality (the idea that everything exists within consciousness alone) is non-limiting. Everything we do, consciously or unconsciously, is to reduce the feeling of being limited. For instance, we might choose to make money in order to be free of debt, pursue a relationship in order to be free of loneliness, or seek entertainment in order to be free of boredom. Therefore, logic would dictate that limitlessness is our very nature. And if limitlessness is our nature, then I am already complete. As a result, I am satisfied (happy).

I am that which enlivens this body-mind. Because of my light shining on it, the body-mind thinks, feels, and knows.

The light is and always was me. I have now completely erased any separation between me and God. There is no distinction; the "union" is complete. Like an electrical current powering an appliance, I give life to this body-mind made up of inert parts.

I am not a part, product or property of the body-mind because the body-mind is an object known to me.

The witness is the unmoving constant that watched the body be born, become an adult, and later, enter into its twilight years. It's also that which will watch the body's imminent death. Because the Self is the witness of change, it cannot be change itself. Seeing this subject-object separation is an important step toward realizing God 1.

I am the subject for all objects, which is anything other than me. All objects are therefore known to me but do not know me.

All objects known to me are inert, including subtle objects such as thoughts. They appear on the screen of consciousness due to an inscrutable force. Because all objects known to me are inert, they cannot know me, only I can know them. All objects exist within me but are not me.

I am the existence, nature and essence of all objects. The consciousness that I am, is the same consciousness because of

which the universe exists.

All objects come out of consciousness and resolve back into it. As the ground of all existence, objects are dependent on me. This is a cognitive shift that shows objects are not "out there," they are in me (consciousness). While this seems counterintuitive and implausible, take the example of a dream. In a dream you are the subject, the people, the objects, the trees, the mountains, the sky—everything. You are both the dream intelligence and the dream material. There is nothing you are not! A dream seems real while you're in it, it's only when the dreamer becomes a waker that one understands it was only a dream. Another way to see that everything is consciousness is by contemplating the location of objects. If I stand in front of a building, the building appears to be separate from me until I ask where the experience of the building takes place. If we analyze the process of experience, we find that all experience is a thought occurring in consciousness. If that's true, how far is the building from me? Therefore, everything experienced is the same consciousness because of which the universe exists.

All objects depend on me to exist, but I do not depend on them. I never enter the world even though it reflects me—just as the reflection in a mirror is the same but not the same as the one who casts it.

Me and the material world co-exist but in different orders of reality. Just like a desert never has actual contact with a mirage, I never have actual contact with the world. In other words, what happens to the world doesn't affect me. God 1 is never "contaminated" by the world, because if that were the case, God 1 would not be attributeless, limitless or non-dual. In the Bhagavata Purana, the son of a great sage declares to a king:

O king! No true connection can exist between the objects of the world and the Self. It is only an illusion cast over the Self which makes this seem to appear. This is just like one who observes objects in a dream—there is no actual connection between the objects and the dreamer. (2.9.1)

I am not limited by the boundaries of the body. There is nowhere I am not.

Because the essence of what I am is God's essence, I am not limited by the boundaries of the body. In the simile of the wave, the wave is shown to be just a name and form (mithya), while in reality its essence is just water (satya). The wave comes and goes but the water remains. Another example is the space contained within a pot. Where does the space contained within the pot go once the pot is broken? Nowhere, nor does it "merge" with other space because space is omnipresent and already pervades everything. In the same way, we say consciousness (Brahman) pervades everything.

I am not affected by the death of the body. I am unborn and undying.

In the Bhagavad Gita, Krishna compares the Self to a person who changes their worn-out clothes:

Just as a person gives up their worn-out clothes and puts on new ones, so the embodied Self gives up the bodies of the old and enters into new ones. (2.22)

I am the indivisible, all-pervasive space-like consciousness in which all bodies appear, including the one I refer to as "mine."

I am that which accommodates all objects and experience. God 1 is often compared with space, its closest comparison, due to its omnipresent and immutable nature.

I am not limited by space or time because space and time are objects known to me.

Again, I (the subject) cannot be that which is known by me.

I am that which comes before space and time, both of which are just concepts in duality.

I am self-evident and need nothing to prove my existence. It is obvious all living beings are conscious, though it is not obvious to most that their nature is me, unlimited consciousness.

Due to ignorance and its ability to conceal, our true essence is hidden. Due to its other ability to project, we identify with that which we aren't—namely the body-mind. This ignorance is hardwired, but with Self-inquiry and discrimination is surmountable.

I am always experiencing consciousness and am never not consciousness, even when the body dies.

Even in deep sleep when the mind has temporarily retreated and is unaware of objects or "me," I am still experiencing consciousness via the causal body (sub-conscious). Otherwise, I wouldn't, for example, wake up every time the neighbor's dog starts barking.

I am never in contact with thoughts and experience and am always free of and unaffected by both, though without me, no thought or experience is possible. I illumine and pervade every thought and exist between thoughts. I do not come and go as thoughts come and go. I am the knower of the coming and going of thoughts.

Thoughts can be compared to the individual frames of an old film reel. Like the individual celluloid frames, our world is made up of a sequence of thoughts being played one after the other (try having two thoughts at the same time!). It's this rapid and seamless sequence of thoughts that creates and animates the world for us. So, thoughts make the world but they don't make me (the screen on which thoughts appear and disappear).

Thoughts and experience are subtle objects. No experience happens without me, but I never experience anything. I am the non-experiencing witness of the experiencing entity, the person. No experience takes place "in" me because there is nothing but me.

I am the non-experiencing witness and thus, I am actionless. What, then, is it that is actually experiencing? The mind. This might seem to contradict what was shown previously but it's just a progression from the realization that I am the witness (the knower), to I am the non-experiencing witness (actionless, non-dual awareness). The difference is subtle. The "knower" is a metaphor for the Self but it doesn't perfectly describe it because it infers action (e.g., knowing). The Self isn't a doer, the person is. If an object is revealed by my knowing, then consciousness is simply that which reveals the knowing. If I raise my hand in the air and ask you what you see, you'll say "your hand" without ever recognizing the light that illuminates my hand. In this analogy, the Self is like the light—it reveals without taking any action.

All objects appear in me, change, and die. But I am the only constant unchanging factor. Without me, no object can exist, but I need nothing because I am existence itself.

Like the screen and the movie, I am immutable no matter the objects projected on the screen. I am present before and after the objects appear. All objects appear in me, but I am the only constant unchanging factor. Let the world come and go, I (consciousness) still remain.

Notes

1. Traditionally, the word "consciousness" is used to describe God 1. However, today, consciousness could also be interpreted as the mind or how the mind interprets experience. From Vedanta's perspective the mind and

its workings are just objects projected on the screen of awareness. Nevertheless, I will continue with the traditional format of using "consciousness" to describe pure awareness or absolute reality.

2. Collectively, the Upanishads are Vedanta, or the knowledge summarized at the end of the Vedas that reveal the nature of reality.

3. List adapted from "The Self Is Consciousness," by Sundari Swartz. Commentary is mine. https://www.shiningworld. com/the-self-is-consciousness/

Chapter 2

God 2

If God 1 is the formless consciousness principle, then God 2 as the creative principle is everything we experience, including all objects. In contrast to the monotheistic religions, which suggest God 2 is a benevolent but exasperated elderly male living in an undisclosed location, the Vedic vision tells us God is both the material and efficient cause of creation, which means there is no distance between God and creation—God is creation. This understanding clears up a whole host of issues associated with the belief in a personal God living outside its creation.

The Shvetashvatara Upanishad refers to God 2 when it declares:

> The self-luminous Lord, who is in fire, who is in water, who has entered into the whole world, who is in plants, who is in trees—to that Lord I offer my reverence. (2.17)

God 2 is never bound by personhood, location, space or time. God 2 is limitless, otherwise it would be confined by the constraints of its own nature and as a result, might show certain human-like tendencies such as irritability, fickleness and proneness to error. As much as we enjoy thinking of God 2 as a super-human with likes and dislikes, God 2 doesn't offer up any opinions or take sides. Perhaps a more accurate but less endearing way to think of God 2 is as an intelligent, self-organizing system with rules, patterns and symbiotic relationships that ensures the Total operates in perfect order. As participants in God's universe, it is our job to understand where and how we fit into the system so that we can live in harmony with it and avoid whatever suffering that results from being ignorant of God's ways.

At a visceral level, we might recognize God 2 as the life force felt on a moment-to-moment basis. In the dialogue between the sage and the atheist, the sage creates an immediately relatable picture of God by asking the atheist:

What is it that right now is circulating your blood, telling you that you're hungry, and putting thoughts in your head? What is it that's growing everything — the grass, the flowers, the trees, even the hair on your head?

The sage isn't pointing to some supernatural phenomenon but instead, common everyday occurrences. He's also demonstrating that in spite of all appearances, we aren't actually doing any of these things. In fact, once examined closely, we find our sense of doership is constructed on weak scaffolding and easily toppled by simple observation. Any notion that we are in control turns out to be an illusion, so let's start there.

Vedanta has a method for showing that which conceals our essence called "the teaching of the five sheaths." This method of negation is common in Vedanta which, as a tradition, prefers to describe itself as a means for removing ignorance rather than a means for gaining knowledge. The reason is because you already are what you seek, you just need to remove that which obscures the truth so that you can live satisfied, knowing you're the Self and not the limited individual you think you are.[1]

The five sheaths are presented from grossest to most subtle and figuratively, are situated within each other like an onion so that the most subtle of the sheaths is that which is most hidden. They are called "sheaths" because they are that which hides one's true essence. The more subtle the sheath, the more luminosity the Self is able to manifest so that the grossest of the sheaths is the most "opaque" and the subtlest, the most "translucent." Lastly, it's important to note that each sheath is insentient by nature and not operable by itself.

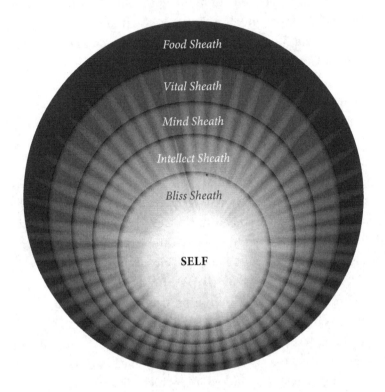

The first sheath is the physical body. Vedanta shows we cannot be the body because if that were the case we would be able to choose, for example, to never get sick, grow old or die. It is called the "food sheath" because the body is formed and maintained via the nutrients it receives from food.

Next, is the vital sheath which is our physiology or life force. This is what the sage is referring to when he asks the atheist what is it that's circulating his blood and telling him that he's hungry. This sheath is responsible for action, hunger and thirst.

Third, we inquire about the mind sheath asking, as the sage does, what is it that puts thoughts in our head? The mind is responsible for will—the faculty on which a person initiates an action. Feelings and emotions also fall within the mind sheath.

The fourth sheath is the intellect—that which calculates, strategizes and reveals solutions. We can't be the intellect either, because if we were it would always remain sharp even when we feel tired, ill or have ingested certain substances (i.e., medication, alcohol, or recreational drugs). The intellect sheath is responsible for knowledge.

Lastly, is the bliss sheath. It's a bit more complicated, but it mostly represents the pleasure from deep sleep when the mind is dormant and there is the absence of any pain or suffering. It is also briefly experienced when one comes in contact with an agreeable or desirable object. The bliss sheath is the most subtle of the sheaths that conceal the Self.

Upon analyzing the five sheaths, the conclusion is that I can't be any of them, not only for the reasons already listed, but because they are all found to be objects known to me. And because they are known to me and are not me (the subject), I can't claim to have absolute control over them. After all, I don't *do* the body and its physiology. I don't *do* my involuntary thoughts or any of the intellect's revelations, and I don't *do* blissful sleep. Although it seems I influence each, in reality they all just happen by a power unbeknownst to me.

As we peel back the onion of personhood more and more, we find there really isn't any doer to be found and that whatever we imagine ourselves to be, is just a story the ego likes to tell itself. And as spooky as that sounds now, it might also come as a relief. If I'm not the doer, God must be the doer because God is the owner of everything. That means I'm off the hook! I must still play by the rules, but I needn't suffer from all "my" perceived imperfections, including my imperfect body and imperfect mind.

In the Bhagavad Gita, God as Krishna describes himself to Arjuna as:

Earth, water, fire, air, space, mind, intellect and even the sense of doership—such is my nature divided eight-fold. (7.4)

He further adds:

Arjuna, I am the taste in water. I am the light in the moon and the sun. I am "Om" in all the Vedas. I am the sound in space, and I am the strength in human beings. I am the sweet fragrance in the earth and the brilliance and heat in fire. I am the very life in all beings, and the austerity in the ascetics. Know me as the one who is the eternal seed in all beings. I am the intelligence in the intelligent and the brilliance in the brilliant... (7.8–11)

In a crushing blow to the ego, Krishna explains that not only is he all the basic constituents that make up the world, but that he's the strength, intelligence, and the "very life in all beings." The doer has now been reduced to a mere actor in the "mind" of God.

In the same verse, Krishna is also describing his nature as that which includes both the material cause and the intelligent cause of the universe, or combined, what I'm calling God 2. The word for God 2 in Sanskrit[2] is *saguna Brahman,* or "God with attributes," and constitutes the lower nature of God's two-fold nature (the higher nature being pure consciousness). But for simplicity, we'll stick with God 2.

According to Vedic cosmology, the material world is made up of the five basic elements Krishna mentions (earth, water, fire, air, space),[3] which is really just a simple way of explaining the principle building blocks of creation and all their various amalgams that result in objects such as stars, trees, bodies, and even iPhones. As the material cause, God 2 is involved in the formation of the most subtle form of matter called *prakriti* ("that which can be molded into manifold objects") used to create the universe and all its various objects. And yet, when we look at any of God's objects, we find evidence of not only matter, but of an intelligent cause that provides creation with structure, relationships and laws.

The Intelligent Cause

Vedanta says the world is not separate from its intelligent cause, but how can God 2 be both the maker and the material? For example, a carpenter can't be both the intelligent and material cause of his work. We don't take home the carpenter when we purchase a new set of table and chairs! So then, how do we reason that God is both the maker and material of the world?

Taking a cue from nature, Vedanta has an elegant way to show how this is possible. In the Mundaka Upanishad it states:

As the spider produces its silk and absorbs it again, as herbs grow from the soil, and as hair grows on man, so does creation spring forth from that which is immutable. (1.1.8)

Here we have mention of the spider which creates a web out of itself. The spider is both the web's material and the intelligence behind it. The silk material the spider uses to construct a web is both extracted and retracted from its mouth, giving it the ability to lower itself down from a single thread or retract itself by consuming it. The material is the spider, but the spider isn't the material. This analogy also shows that while the creation comes out of God, God doesn't become its creation. Nevertheless, like the ability to see the spider from the web, we can see the cause in the effect of creation. Thus, if we are a product of God and endowed with God-given intelligence, we can presume God is the intelligent cause.

When we turn on a computer, although it appears to have a mind of its own and beautifully follow through with its tasks, we know it's only able to do so because a programmer provided the algorithms necessary for it to carry out certain functions.

Similarly, when we look at something in nature such as an acorn, we might also see it as having a "program" that knows perfectly how to grow the acorn into a towering oak. So an acorn is much more than just its material, it's embedded knowledge.

As another example, science tells us that objects are made up of molecular particles. As interesting as it is that these particles even exist, is their ability to "stick" by exerting subatomic forces on each other and forming everything from planets and stars to the amazing complexity of the human body, let alone a brain capable of reading and understanding these words. But how do you get from inert matter to, let's say, human beings sending themselves to the moon?

What both of these examples implies is an intelligent cause. So, God is not only all of existence, but the logic behind existence. The whole universe has been meticulously brought forth. Scientists have theories on how species have evolved and how they have come up with clever, never-seen-before methods for ensuring their continuation. For example, Darwin's theory of evolution (now, scientific orthodoxy) by natural selection dictates that the reason for the giraffe's long neck is due to variants that occurred in its genetic code. Some of these variants subtly changed the bones and muscles in the ancestors of the giraffe allowing it to reach higher branches, eat more leaves and accumulate better nutrition. As a result of this advantage, giraffes with the long neck attribute were able to produce more offspring and eventually dominate their species. Thus, the underlying theme of natural selection says that gene variants are the cause of the successful evolution of a species.[4] And this theory of evolution makes sense—up to a point. Where it falls off is when we seek to understand not only the evolution of life but the origin of it. How is it that from some dead material that you get self-sustaining cells capable of processing information and replicating themselves, let alone making entire organisms?

Throughout history, scientists and philosophers have been

accustomed to explaining creation via the concept of cause and effect. But even that takes us only so far. Just like you can't make a cake with only flour, common sense would tell us you can't make a universe with only hydrogen (the most abundant element in the universe) or expect it to make itself using only dynamic fields (the method from which particles bond). But hydrogen or no hydrogen, what should be obvious to anyone is that *you can't get something from nothing.* Why there is anything at all is the universe's greatest mystery. We can deduce that the dog came from the wolf and that humans came from the ape, but it defeats all logic to conclude that the universe came from nothing at all. So, while it may be easy to argue that there is no personal God sitting in the clouds benevolently looking down on us, it's unreasonable to argue that there is no intelligent cause and that the universe put itself together based on chance and, well, one thing leading to another.

But the point of all this isn't to definitively prove the existence of a cosmic architect but instead show that super-intelligence is built into the system. For as much as we'd like to believe that science will someday find an answer to every mystery, it's hard to believe that life isn't without purpose — even if that purpose is simply to know itself. It's a bit of a paradox because science (defined as the method for testing hypotheses using empirical evidence) continues to show us with each new discovery, how a particular aspect of the cosmos is the way it is, but at the same time any grand unified theory[5] to explain it all seems ever-elusive (in spite of all those alluring science book titles purporting otherwise). This might be due to the observation that in nature every explanation requires a further explanation, which requires another, and another, ad infinitum. Or as the sage tells the atheist, "Open one door and there's another, and another — an endless succession of doors to be opened."

Even if some day we were somehow able to arrive at an answer to every scientific question, how could one ever stop wondering how it all seamlessly works together to create *this*? Just because we fully understand how a cell works doesn't mean we're no longer left in complete awe over the improbability of something on such a small scale working with almost perfect efficiency. To take it all for granted and just say, "Well, you know, that's nature for you!" seems to be naive at best. Fortunately, there are scientists who still believe the natural world is not just a banal arrangement of entities and forces but rather, a kind of ingenious and unified scheme. But a scheme set by what?

One reason why pursuing the idea that there is a cosmic architect doesn't get us anywhere is because we can never prove a first cause to the universe or show that a super-being created and orchestrates the universe based on a grand plan. In the end, any talk about there being a universal patriarch can only ever be a personal belief. Does that go against what, previously, the sage was trying to show the atheist? No, because it's only human to want to put a name to a face—in this case, the face of creation.

From Vedanta's point of view, God 2 isn't so much an entity as a benign force[6] to understand, appreciate and live in harmony with. Within the Vedic tradition, God is revered because as individuals we are totally dependent on God for everything. But the idea that God is an entity is seen as a personal choice that serves mostly to help facilitate worship. Devotees are encouraged to worship God in a form of their choosing, whether it be Krishna, Shiva, Vishnu; God in the male form or female form; God in the animal form or half-animal/half-human form; or even nature itself. In this way, the devotee is given a simple and attainable means for having a dialogue with the universe. So, God, as a concept, also has the purpose of being a sort of catchall for a mysterious order we can never fully understand. It's a recognition of our place in the bigger picture and a means for developing a special relationship with it.

At the same time, we need to acknowledge that science

isn't always the ultimate decider for what's true. Within the context of theoretical science, it could be argued that science is another belief system. This isn't meant to diminish the importance of science, its process, or suggest that all science is subjective (as some American politicians and clergymen conveniently do). The point is that, in general, science can only ever be an approximation of what we currently know to be true about the material world. Sure, we might trust and be thankful for science every time we receive a vaccination, communicate with loved ones miles away, board an airplane, and the thousand other big and small ways that science has made life easier. But in regards to coherent models, scientists are periodically forced to reconsider their view of the universe.[7] This change is typically led by a single individual whose discovery swaps out the current system for a new one. In the past, individuals such as Copernicus, Newton, and Einstein have been responsible for such change. But even Einstein got things wrong on occasion.[8]

Scientist also still have much to learn about the most common of things, such as space or what exactly distinguishes life from non-life. The fact is many models that were introduced in the twentieth century in order to impart a greater picture of the cosmos will most likely be modified or replaced even within our own lifetime. Furthermore, the laws of nature put strict limits on what humans can and can't learn about the universe. We can't ever look inside black holes or peer any further into the distance than light has traveled since the start of the Big Bang, which means that not even 1 percent of the cosmos is visible through our telescopes.

Lastly, scientists can't even agree on what consciousness is—our most fundamental aspect! So, while science is still our best means for understanding the material world, its findings shouldn't be accepted as absolute.[9] Similar to Vedanta, science isn't really about proving things, so much as, disproving them. Science also isn't about gaining direct knowledge of the truth, but instead, about building testable models that predict how the universe behaves. There are some scientific theories that are controversial and others that are quite robust (or as paleontologist Stephen Jay Gould writes, are "confirmed to such a degree that it would be perverse to withhold provisional assent"[10]). It's prudent to keep in mind that science isn't a process that progresses to an absolute and final conclusion but rather, from one stepping stone to the next.

Albert Einstein, who had a "cosmic religious sense" — meaning, he had a profound reverence for the beauty and order of nature — once received a letter from a young girl in the sixth grade who wanted to know if scientists prayed. Thoughtfully, he wrote back:

> Scientific research is based on the idea that everything that takes place is determined by laws of nature, and therefore this holds for the actions of people. For this reason, a research scientist will hardly be inclined to believe that events could be influenced by a prayer, i.e. by a wish addressed to a supernatural being. However, it must be admitted that our actual knowledge of these laws is only imperfect and fragmentary, so that, actually, the belief in the existence of basic all-embracing laws in nature also rests on a sort of faith. All the same this faith has been largely justified so far by the success of scientific research. But, on the other hand, everyone who is seriously involved in the pursuit of science becomes convinced that a spirit is manifest in the laws of the universe — a spirit vastly superior to that of man, and one in the face of which we with our modest powers must feel humble. In this way the pursuit of science leads to a religious feeling of a special sort, which is indeed quite different from the religiosity of someone more naive.[11]

Defining "Creation"

Just as we need to define "God" in order to have a meaningful conversation about God, in order to understand what's knowable and not regarding creation, we need to first define the word "creation." For starters, "creation" is not an accurate description due to the law of conservation which states that matter and energy are never created or destroyed. While name and form may be created and destroyed, matter and energy can only ever be recycled and made into something else. If we burn a log, the log appears to no longer exist but matter and energy still exist as smoke, ash and heat. We can say there is no more log but we can't say there is no-thing. This isn't a belief, it's a fact. Thus, the more appropriate word for the beginning of the world is "manifestation" because there never was and never has been no-thing. So, when we use the word "creation" we should really think of it as manifestation and not as an absolute beginning.

Vedanta suggests that all objects have always existed either in potential or active form. Something that is in potential form doesn't mean that it is non-existent, only that it's not available for perception or transaction. For example, when we look at milk, we don't see butter but we know the butter exists in potential form. So, due to the law of conservation, it makes sense that the cosmos would have existed at another time in a seed state.

The metaphor of the seed representing the unmanifest applies to both the microcosm and the macrocosm. The beauty of this cosmology shows what nature has always shown us—that what we find at the micro level often corresponds with what we find at the macro level and vice versa. In other words, maybe we don't need to experience all of creation to understand it. As the wise like to say, to know the taste of the ocean, one needn't drink the entire ocean! In his conversation with the atheist, the sage tries to make a similar point when he says (with a bit of a sense of humor):

> God's stuff is just patterns, patterns everywhere... and God is very frugal. Take nature's fractals, for example. The veins under your skin appear as the veins in a leaf, which look like the branches of a tree, which appear the same as lightning in the sky, and so on and so on... Nature is just a fixed set of laws with the same patterns applied over and over again. From a few we get the many, just like from the 26 letters of the alphabet we're able to assemble thousands of words, essays and cheap romance novels.

Scientists are continuously looking for the new, but all they really ever find are new combinations of the same. Any real artist would tell you there is no creation, just new and novel ways of putting together the same. Everything in the universe is derivative of something else, which means among us, there are no actual creators, only finders.

Vedanta doesn't equate creation with an absolute beginning but instead, with cycles. In this way, the universe's potential and active states might be thought of as night and day for God 2. Thus, what is thought of as the creation of the world is really the beginning of another cycle. Even scientists are debating whether or not the universe might have an eternal past before the Big Bang. Some cosmological models propose that the universe has gone through endless cycles of expansion and contraction (for which Vedanta would wholly agree!).

So if creation is really manifestation, it's no longer correct to say that God creates the world. It's more accurate to say God *activates* the world, because the world is never actually created or destroyed. It just goes in and out of inactive and active states. (Nevertheless, I'll continue to use "create" and "creation" in the figurative sense.)

Maya

In order to fully understand creation or the cycles of manifestation, we need to first remember the role of God 1 (the formless, consciousness principle) as the substrate on which the active and inactive states of the universe play out. God 1 is the unchanging factor on which the world is repeatedly created, preserved, and destroyed through entropy. However, God 1 has no powers and is actionless, which means it doesn't actually create. So, to use the movie analogy again, if God 1 is the movie screen and isn't the movie, where does the movie come from? What is it that's actually "doing" creation?

To arrive at our answer, we'll first need to define God 2 as the special relationship between consciousness and *maya*. God 1 is consciousness without attributes (*nirguna* Brahman) and God 2 is consciousness with attributes (*saguna* Brahman). The first point to note about this arrangement is that God 2 and all beings, including you and me, share the same essence—consciousness. Just as a person is said to borrow consciousness as the embodied Self, God 2 also borrows consciousness. Therefore, we say God 2 is conscious. However, for both God 2 and individuals, consciousness is made to appear as something it's not.

To illustrate this, the example of a red bottle is used. When water is poured into a red bottle, the water appears to be affected by the redness of the bottle. It's only through the knowledge that colored glass distorts the appearance of its contents that we know the water hasn't actually changed. In the same way, for humans, the body-mind makes consciousness appear to be the five sheaths. As for God 2, it is *maya* which makes consciousness appear to be the world. So to understand the world, we need to understand maya.

Maya cannot be said to be existent or non-existent, nor both; neither same nor different, nor both; neither made up of parts nor whole, nor both. Maya is a great wonder and cannot be categorically explained. (Shankaracharya, *Vivekachudamani*, verse 109)

Maya is not a part of consciousness. If maya were part of consciousness it would affect consciousness because what affects a part affects the whole. Maya is the creative power that makes consciousness appear as name and form (objects). It's an illusory superimposition similar to how a dream is an illusory superimposition to the waker. Unlike the waker who falls under the dream's spell, God 2 wields maya without ever losing control of its powers.

Although God 2 and maya are, for all practical purposes, synonymous, they have different connotations. God 2 is perceived as benefactor, the keeper of laws and cosmic balance, and the giver of the results of action. From a religious perspective, God 2 is available for worship, prayer and devotion. On the other hand, maya is perceived not only as God 2's creative power, but often, figuratively, as a sinister influence that makes living beings forget their identity and relationship with God using its twin powers of concealment and projection. Maya is the power in awareness that seemingly puts us under a spell and has us fail to recognize the actual nature of objects. This is similar to how we become captivated by the forms projected on a movie screen without ever recognizing that the forms are just light. Thus, in addition to being credited with all matters worldly, maya is also credited with being the root cause of ignorance. Nevertheless, in the end, maya serves an important purpose. While maya acts as deluder, it also acts as liberator, because one can only know the transitory and unsatisfactory quality of the world through experience. Ultimately, it's maya that paves the way to the individual's eventual freedom.

Krishna as God's avatar in the Gita reminds us:

Indeed this maya, which belongs to me, which is the modification of the three powers, is difficult to cross. Those who seek only me cross this maya. (7.14)

Maya makes the impossible, possible by having the one appear as the many. How we get an infinite array of objects from consciousness can be illustrated with the example of a gold necklace. With a gold necklace, it is assumed that the gold has become the necklace, but in reality, the gold never changed. If we melt down the necklace, we no longer have the necklace but we still have the gold. So, with some heat we can get rid of the necklace, but we can't get rid of the gold. In fact, we shouldn't call it a gold necklace, we should call it necklace-y gold because "necklace" is only a name and form. Its real essence is gold. One is mithya (apparently real), while the other is satya (the truth). That the "necklace" appears real is an illusion or maya. That one is able to create many different kinds of objects using the same gold—such as earrings, bracelets, rings, cufflinks, etc.—is also maya.

Another example that shows how objects are derived from consciousness is what happens when we dream. As mentioned in the previous chapter, in a dream you are both the subject and the objects; both the intelligent cause and the material cause of your dream. A dream feels real while you're in it, it's only when you have awoken that it is known to have been a dream. Such is the hypnotizing power of maya!

Vedanta is able to explain the *what* of maya (its nature, how it works, what its relationship is to absolute reality, etc.), but it doesn't veer into the *why*. Maya cannot be separated from consciousness in the same way you cannot separate the power of fire to burn from its power to illumine. However, even though maya and consciousness co-exist, they are not the same. While consciousness is the ground of all being, it is actionless and has no attributes. Maya has attributes (which we'll discuss in the next chapter) but is dependent on consciousness. Therefore, from Vedanta's perspective maya isn't *sat* (real) because maya is not always manifest (it comes and goes with the cycles of creation) and can't exist without consciousness. It's also not *asat* (not real) because we experience its effects. The best we can say is that maya is "apparently real" (mithya).

Maya is referred to in many ways, such as the stuff of matter, the material universe, the macrocosmic causal body, and the root of all ignorance. Scientists, in particular, have an endless fascination with maya even if they don't call it by the same name. But Vedanta, instead of trying to explain why maya exists and fall down a rabbit hole from which no one has ever returned, simply categorizes it as inscrutable. The wise advise that analyzing the origins of maya doesn't get us anywhere because maya is like a dream, and to wake from a dream you don't obsess with questions about the dream objects (where they came from and how they came to be). If you're serious about enlightenment (spiritual freedom), they tell us, the objective is to wake up, not become enamored with the dream.

Samsara

Maya, with all its bright shiny objects, keeps us in endless fascination. As beings with a myriad of desires, we are easily seduced by its charms. While all desire isn't inherently bad, maya likes to play to our extreme likes and dislikes and our tendency to become attached to them. Maya works by intelligently projecting the universe while at the same time hiding the truth by using our likes and dislikes to turn our gaze outward. In the Gita, Krishna reveals God's lesser nature that plays to our impulses and holds sway over us when he says:

The Lord remains in the heart of all beings, Arjuna. By its maya it causes them to dance as if they were puppets on a string. (18.61)

As sentient beings with an intellect, we are particularly proficient at creating our own psychological traps. Due to reinforced conditioning, we become so infatuated with certain objects that it becomes unclear if we have control of the object or if the object has control of us. Maya puts us under its spell by taking our object of desire and hiding its negative aspects, while at the same time emphasizing or exaggerating its positive ones. This causes us to misinterpret reality, leading us to suffer when the desire turns into addiction or when the pleasure we assumed would last forever, comes to an abrupt end. The only way to escape maya's spell is via vigilance, knowledge, and constant discrimination. So, at the individual and psychological level, maya is synonymous with the fundamental ignorance that keeps us from seeing reality as it is.

Maya is a great magician and as individuals without knowledge of it, we are its captive audience. For example, one of maya's amazing tricks is the illusion that joy is in objects. Logic tells us that objects by themselves are value neutral and incapable of emanating or giving happiness. If this weren't the case, every object that gives me joy would give you joy too. Because we know this not to be true, it means the happiness you experience must be originating from you and not the object. And yet, we scour the earth pursuing various objects and relationships in hope that objects, including relationships, will fulfill us. The result is often disappointment as we discover that whatever we thought would indelibly satisfy us, in the long run, turns out to be empty of any lasting pleasure.

This negative psychological condition brought on by the misinterpretation of reality is called *samsara*.[12] A *samsari* is a person who believes the material world is the source of true happiness and who is willing to suffer the effect of constant disillusionment until convinced otherwise (usually after many years, perhaps lifetimes). So, maya produces many beautiful experiences for us to enjoy, but none worth growing attached to.[13] Thus, if maya is the cause of our delusion, *samsara* is surely the effect.

A Causeless Cause

We can come up with all kinds of theories about why God created the world. Perhaps God created the world for sport, or simply to observe its own splendor. This question is, of course, open to many interpretations. And while it's fun to speculate why God created the world, it doesn't get us anywhere. However, regarding the question of an absolute beginning to the world, Vedanta is decisive when it says there is none. What came first, the chicken or the egg? Or in the case of the world—the cause or the effect? It's the kind of question that has no answer. Our error is that we always imagine creation happening at a particular time and place. As we already know, matter can never be created or destroyed, and the world can only exist in either potential or active form. Thus, the question of whether or not there is a first cause is moot. In spite of what religion says, logic would tell us God 1 can't be a first cause because God 1 is actionless, and God 2 can't be a first cause because of the law of conservation. Nevertheless, we still experience creation and cause and effect. Such is this inscrutable maya!

Notes

1. According to Christian doctrine, all individuals are born sharing the sinfulness of Adam and Eve's first disobedience to God in the Garden of Eden. This is what is referred to as "original sin." In Vedanta, there is no concept of original sin. However, there is beginningless ignorance (cosmic maya), which has the effect of concealing and distancing one's relationship with God until such a time that the ignorance is removed.

2. Throughout this book I have tried to minimize the use of Sanskrit in an effort to not make things more complicated than

need be. Nevertheless, certain Sanskrit words are necessary to describe concepts not easily translated into English. Like any science, Vedanta or the "science of consciousness" (as some like to describe it) has its own jargon to help express technical concepts in precise terminology. Using specific Sanskrit words also helps to put cumbersome terminology into shorthand. Sanskrit terms can be quite nuanced with multiple meanings depending on the context. For more on Vedanta's usage of basic Sanskrit terms, I recommend reading *Tattva Bodha* by the eighth-century expounder of Vedanta, Shankaracharya.

3. The Greeks similarly believed that all matter was made up of a handful of elements (in their case, just four, not including space). Scientists today talk of the universe consisting of just three elementary particles: the "up" quark, the "down" quark, and the electron.

4. Vedanta has no qualms about science's evolution theory or description of the material world. Where it is in conflict is in science's presumption that consciousness evolved out of matter. Using logic, Vedanta shows that what we experience as being "out there" actually exists in consciousness and that consciousness is the root of all experience. Meanwhile, science struggles to understand how, from a gray, jelly-like lump of tissue and neurons, we get consciousness.

5. While scientists vigorously hunt for a grand unified theory, Vedanta says you needn't look any further than your Self within which the whole world exists.

6. God is viewed as benign because it's only due to our ignorance that we suffer or fear anything at all.

7. Scientists in the past have been forced to change their views. Such examples include, Earth as the center of the universe, the absolute nature of time and space, the stability of continents, and the cause of infectious disease (Oreskes, Naomi. "If You Say 'Science Is Right,' You're Wrong."

Scientific American. July 1, 2021).

8. Einstein, at first, refused to accept that the universe was expanding, instead arguing that the universe was closed and static. He also refused to concede that communication between quantum particles could travel across space faster than light, as that would violate the law of special relativity.

9. Not even scientists accept all their conclusions as absolute, as that would go against their credo, which is to exhaust any and all uncertainty.

10. Gould, Stephen Jay. *Hen's Teeth and Horse's Toes: Further Reflections in Natural History*. W.W. Norton & Co., 1983. p.255.

11. Einstein, Albert. *Albert Einstein, the Human Side: New Glimpses from His Archives*. Princeton University Press. p.32.

12. The word "samsara" has various meanings, all of which are related to being bound, trapped or limited. For more about samsara, see my book, *Samsara: An Exploration of the Hidden Forces that Shape and Bind Us*.

13. As it turns out, the secret to leading a happy life isn't the getting and keeping of objects, but knowing when to let go of them!

Chapter 3

Creator, Sustainer, Destroyer

God 2 is not only the creator, but also the sustainer and destroyer of the world. In Hindu mythology, these cosmic roles are represented by the three deities, Brahma (creator), Vishnu (preserver) and Shiva (destroyer).[1] In spite of what appears to be polytheism, each deity actually represents an aspect of the one God and serves as a reminder of God's universal powers. The idea that God be worshipped equally as creator, sustainer and destroyer might seem strange to westerners who were brought up with the belief that God is a benevolent entity that lives outside of his creation. However, it makes sense that God should be equally worshipped as creator, sustainer and destroyer. The whole universe is dependent on various cycles of destruction and renewal for its existence. We see it in the astronomical events of supernovae, in the seasons on Earth, and even within our own bodies which replaces itself with a new set of cells every 7–10 years. All of these events can be attributed to God's governance of the universe via creation, sustainment and dissolution.

Most devotees tend to ignore the less savory side of God. When God is known through the heart, God's universal form as the various appalling and destructive forces of nature is muted. This makes God caring, loving and approachable as Father, Mother, friend, companion or beloved. For lovers of God (*bhaktas*), these qualities are preferred over God's impersonal attributes and ineffable form. Such a devotee chooses to worship a personal God through love only.

But regardless of how we choose to view God, the fact is the universe is a non-stop self-perpetuating machine that is constantly creating the new and dismantling and recycling the old. To disregard this ravaging aspect of God is to deny life itself. When we say "no" to all the wasting and horrors of the world and demand that it be otherwise, we are in a sense saying that we know better than God. We may wish life didn't include such things as death, disease, and violence, but life is what it is. We must work within God's order and acknowledge the truth that all life is driven by a fixed set of laws, including the fundamental instincts of self-propagation and self-preservation.

There's a related story about Shiva from the Puranas, who comes by a monster that insists on taking his bride as his mistress. To remove the annoyance, Shiva shoots a burst of power from his third eye that creates a horrendous and ravenous lion. The monster, taking a quick measure of the situation, begs Shiva for mercy. In Hindu lore there are certain rules that even the gods must abide by, so Shiva is obligated to grant the monster mercy. However, the emaciated lion is still hungry and unsatisfied. So, finding no other way to resolve the problem, Shiva suggests that the lion satisfy its hunger by eating itself! Thus, the ravenous lion begins with its tail and proceeds to work up its body until only the upper part of its face remains. Shiva, utterly charmed by the result, dubs the monster *Kirtimukha*, "The Face of Glory," and declares that it should always be placed at the door of his shrines. Thus, Kirtimukha becomes a symbol of Shiva himself. Joseph Campbell tells a similar version of this story and describes it as the perfect image of the ferocity of life whose nature is to eat itself.[2] The challenge, as Campbell explains it, is to put yourself in agreement with world— not as you think it should be, but as it is.

Another Hindu mythological example of nature's destructive power is the Kali-like goddess Chinnamasta (Sanskrit for "she whose head is severed"). Chinnamasta is seen as the fearsome aspect of the Divine Mother (the feminine aspect of creation), symbolizing both life-giver and life-taker. The ghastly Chinnamasta is depicted naked, standing on a copulating couple, spewing blood from her self-decapitated head which she holds to nourish her attendants. The violent and shocking image is the epitome of nature's combined destructive and recreative powers, symbolized by both the devoured and the devourer. Chinnamasta represents the brutal realization that in order to continue and prosper, life must consume life.

In another example, in the Bhagavad Gita Krishna gives Arjuna a divine eye in order to show him his universal form which includes not only his awesome self-effulgent part, but his universal, savage and destructive one. Arjuna describes what he sees:

> Krishna, the mighty armed, having seen your astonishing form of endless mouths and eyes, of many arms, thighs, feet and stomachs, and rows of fearsome teeth, those who observe are afraid and indeed, so am I. (11.23)

Uneasy, Arjuna continues narrating the graphic scene before him:

> Just like many swollen rivers flowing toward the ocean at once, so do these heroes in the world of men enter your flaming mouths. Just as moths hastily enter a blazing fire to meet their demise, so too, these people enter your mouths at great speed to their own destruction. Devouring all the people on every side with your fiery flaming mouths, you savor it, licking again and again. Your fiery flames fill and scorch the entire universe with their burning radiance! (11.29–30)

Like a scene from a Goya painting, Arjuna describes a God that sadistically enjoys the consumption of his own creation, indifferent to the violence. The Lord, soon after, compares his destructive force with the ruinous quality of time itself, which eventually dissolves all forms into oblivion. He declares:

I am time, the world-destroyer of people, the one who is found in all places, whose activity is to make people age and die....(11.32)

Shaking like a leaf, Arjuna begs God to return back to his avatar form:

I rejoice in having the privilege to see what has never been seen before, and yet, my mind is troubled with fear. Please only show me that previous form of yours, O Lord of the gods! (11.45)

The great warrior, Arjuna is fearful because he has not included his formless Self in the cosmic vision—that which is apart from the creative and destructive forces of the universe.

All objects, from the smallest microbe to the tallest mountain and even planets, are born, sustained for some time and eventually, cease to be. And yet, the story of the universe isn't so much about creation and destruction or a beginning and an end, as it is about transformation. Everything in the universe is on its way to becoming something else and because of the law of conservation, nothing is ever really lost. Even within our own bodies, we find traces of forms that once were something else. Carl Sagan was fond of saying our bodies are literally the stuff of stars,[3] including the iron in our blood, the calcium in our teeth and the nitrogen in our DNA. In fact, it can be said that all objects are just recycled parts!

No other aspect of nature symbolizes this more than the mighty atom which is so vigorously recycled and distributed throughout the cosmos that it has been theorized that each of us carries within us atoms that once passed through millions of other organisms including such historical figures as Buddha, Genghis Khan, William Shakespeare or any other historical personality you can think of. While this realization might not provide any comfort to the feeble ego, who never tires of reminding itself of its uniqueness in the universe, as enlightened individuals we can relax because we literally have nothing to lose except the erroneous belief that we are separate entities apart from the rest of the cosmos.

How nature is able to take some debris from the explosion of early stars, have it grow two legs and make it walk on the surface of a planet is still, for the most part, baffling. Nevertheless, as beings who prefer creation and longevity over destruction and death, it's only natural that we should ponder less about the end of the world, and more about its creation and preservation. Thus, the rest of this chapter is dedicated to the creative aspect of God and how it's proposed that from a few basic elements we get a world full of diverse objects and sentiency.

Before continuing, it should be noted that although the course of events outlined below includes some surprising parallels with modern cosmology, it is not meant to be a scientific explanation of creation. Instead, it shows how, according to the ancient seers, maya borrows existence from consciousness in order to evolve the world from a seed state. It also categorizes the basic constituents of the universe in a way that, while not current with our scientific standards, is delightfully elegant in its depiction. In the end, the objective is to show that all things come out of and resolve back into God as Brahman (pure consciousness).

The Stages of Manifestation

(In the beginning)
There was neither existence nor nonexistence,
All this world was unmanifested energy...
The One breathed, without breath, by its own power
Nothing else was there...

—Excerpt from the *Rig Veda*, circa 1700 BCE

According to scripture, the manifestation of the universe takes place in four stages coming out of the beginningless causal universe (the unmanifested seed state). Before going into the details, it's helpful to briefly outline the process of creation:

In the unmanifest state, God 2 is the eternal knower of the forces, laws and structure of creation. Out of the **causal universe** comes the first stage of manifestation, which is the evolution of the invisible five subtle elements: space, air, fire, water, and earth. In the next stage, from the five subtle elements is created the **subtle universe**. In the third stage, there is the evolution of the five basic elements into their physical and tangible counterparts. In the final stage, the **gross universe** is formed from the combination and recombination of the five gross elements into objects.

So, out of the causal universe, we get the formation of the subtle universe and gross universe. And while the causal universe has no beginning, the subtle and gross universes do. As its name implies, the causal universe is the cause of the subtle universe, and the subtle universe is the cause of the gross universe. When the time of cosmic dissolution arrives and the cycle ends, all gross and subtle objects merge back into the causal universe in the reverse order from which they evolved. This is what is sometimes referred to as "the big cosmic sleep," or what science likes to call the "Big Crunch.[4]" Thus, continues the cycle of creation from the unmanifest to the manifest, and back again.

Let's begin unpacking the stages of manifestation from the beginning, which includes Brahman (in this case, consciousness as a cosmological entity) lending existence to maya. This works similarly to how electricity lends existence to your computer's desktop. As explained earlier, Brahman plus maya is referred to as God 2. Brahman is sometimes referred to as the Universal Father and maya, the Universal Mother. Together, they represent the two parts that make creation possible.

In the Gita, Krishna declares:

Arjuna, my maya is the primordial cause of which I impregnate and which everything grows and is sustained. From that occurs the manifestation of all beings. The great maya is the original material cause for those forms which are born in all wombs, and I am the father who gives the seed. (14.3–4)

Of course, this is all figurative but makes the point that neither Brahman or maya by themselves make the world. It takes two to tango.

Universal Forces

So far, we've described the beginning of the manifestation from the point of view of Brahman as pure consciousness, and maya as the five basic elements. Next, we're going to introduce the powers of maya, which will help complete the picture.

The causal universe or "cosmic maya" is the undifferentiated state of pure potentiality that includes the blueprints for all creation. Maya is a collective made up of three faculties. These faculties, or powers, together are referred to in Sanskrit as the *gunas* and include: *rajas, tamas* and *sattva*. In addition, each guna has its own set of characteristics which differentiates its role in the creation from the other.

Rajas is the power of action and motion that causes objects in nature to move and interact. In terms of physics, rajas might be thought of as the four fundamental forces: gravitation, electromagnetism, and the weak and strong nuclear forces. Tamas is inertia or matter, the actual physical substance that forms the universe. At its most basic level, it might be thought of as the atom and its smaller components: nuclei, protons and neutrons, and quarks. Lastly, sattva is order, balance and knowledge. For example, sattva might be thought of as the information component evident in the datum found in life's genetic code. Scientists are now beginning to recognize that information is to be found even at the quantum level in the form of electrons spinning up or down similar to the binary code a computer uses.[5] The takeaway is that even at the most elementary level, the universe consists of knowledge. Thus, due to the gunas we are able to say everything in nature is related by knowledge-energy-matter. This aligns with some scientists who now, along with energy and matter, have added information as a third essential universal concept.

All chemical changes and even the evolution of life itself are born from the gunas. The three gunas also form the components of each of the five basic elements. For example, space has a rajas component, a tamas component and a sattva component. The same applies to the other four elements: air, fire, water and earth. With the five basic elements and the gunas as the universal building blocks, we can now expand our view of the creation of the universe.

Like any birth, the universe is said to have manifested from seed form.[6] The great essence of the universe is kept in seed form as cosmic knowledge. At the beginning of the manifestation of the universe, the subtle universe or "cosmic mind" arises from pure sattva, which provides the knowledge as well as the cognitive function of self-awareness. God 2 is conscious, not in the sense that God 2 has a physical brain, but in that it is aware, intelligent and omniscient.

To form the universe, the first task is the creation of space by the action of the gunas. It's interesting to note that scripture— which has existed for thousands of years—refers to space as an element. This might seem to contradict our actual experience, but as Einstein showed us in the last century, space is not to be considered something totally distinct from matter but instead, as a material-like component that bends, flexes and undulates.

After the creation of space, the subtle elements are born in sequence: from subtle space is born subtle air (gas); from subtle air is born subtle fire (heat); from subtle fire is born subtle water (liquid); and from subtle water is born subtle earth (matter). "Born" is used figuratively here, because no new elements are actually created due to the law of conservation. Everything is derivative from the gunas, which, in themselves, are inscrutable.

The third and fourth stages involve the creation of objects. Through a process of amalgamation and the predominance of *tamoguna*, the subtle basic elements gradually combine and recombine by increasing densities to become gross elements. The gross elements then form to become compounds based on measured proportions of each of the subtle elements. If we wish to describe the early stages of creation in terms of physics, we might say the combination of the space element along with energy from rajas produces vibrations. Because of the friction caused by the vibrations, there is intense heat (fire element). From the heat comes liquid (water element) which is then, condensed into gross matter (earth element).

This grossification of the elements into matter occurs with each subtle element dividing into two halves. One half is left intact while the other half is divided into four sections with each of the four sections containing one of the four remaining subtle elements. For example, space consists of one-half portion of subtle space plus another half that is one-eighth each of subtle air, fire, water and earth. The other half of space is then distributed to the other four elements, so that one-eighth goes to air, one-eighth goes to fire, one-eighth goes to water, and one-eight goes to earth.

Stage of grossification	Space (1)	Air (2)	Fire (3)	Water (4)	Earth (5)	Process
Stage 1	■	■	■	■	■	Each element is in its original form
Stage 2	▣	▣	▣	▣	▣	Each element splits into two
Stage 3	▦ 2 3 4 5	▦ 1 3 4 5	▦ 1 2 4 5	▦ 1 2 3 5	▦ 1 2 3 4	One half remains intact while the other half gets divided into four equal parts representing 1/8 portion of each of the other elements

Thus, before grossification each element is pure, and after grossification each element is an alloy or a combination of the five elements with one element predominant. From there, the five gross elements combine and recombine to form objects.

Below is a summary of the four stages of manifestation showing the role of the gunas and the basic elements.

Stage of manifestation	Role of the gunas	Elements involved	State of manifestation
Stage 1	Out of the causal universe and with the help of the gunas, evolve the **subtle five basic elements**	Subtle elements	Subtle universe
Stage 2	Out of pure sattvaguna evolves the **subtle universe** or blueprint for how to create the universe	Subtle elements	Subtle universe
Stage 3	From the gunas predominate by tamas, evolve the **five gross elements**	Gross elements	Gross universe
Stage 4	Out of the combination and recombination of the five gross elements evolve **objects**	Gross elements	The Totality (combined causal, subtle and gross universes)

The Macrocosmic and Microcosmic

The macrocosmic and the microcosmic are both terms used to separate the manifestation of the world (Total) from the manifestation of the person (individual). However, there is no intrinsic difference between the macrocosm and the microcosm. In short, the microcosm is a reflection of the macrocosm. Both are made up of the same five elements and both include three bodies (gross, subtle and causal). Another way to think of this it is as the difference between the forest and a tree in the forest. Either can be perceived as a single entity.

The macrocosm is God 2, or consciousness under the influence of maya which projects the world and conceals Brahman. Maya makes Brahman appear to be something different than it is. On the other hand, when we speak of the microcosmic, we're referring to the body-mind-sense complex of the apparent individual afflicted with Self-ignorance. The ignorance is due to maya, that is, the person's subjective interpretation of reality colored by the psychological aspect of the gunas. It's for this reason that maya is defined both as the material universe and as the root of ignorance. On the other hand, God 2 never comes under the influence of its maya, just as a magician never comes under the influence of his own magic.

The three powers, or gunas, make up not only the gross, physical body of the individual but—as the process of creation shows—the subtle body (mind-intellect-ego) as well. This means that for the individual, even thoughts are objects and derived from the gunas. In other words, the powers that make our outer world also make our inner world, with both outer and inner worlds existing as objects known to me (the Self).

Out of the same subtle elements that manifest the macrocosm, are manifested different parts of the microcosm or the individual's subtle body, including the five sense organs, the five organs of action, the five vital organs and the inner organ made up of four functions.

Organ Type	Function	Guna
Five sense organs	Hearing, touch, sight, taste, smell	Sattva
Inner organ	Mind, intellect, ego, memory	Sattva
Five organs of action	Speech, hands, legs, anus, genitals	Rajas
Five vital organs	Respiration, excretion, circulation, digestion, ejection	Rajas

From the sattva aspect of each of the five subtle elements are formed the **five sense organs**.

- From subtle **space** is born the organ of **hearing**
- From subtle **air** is born the organ of **touch**
- From subtle **fire** is born the organ of **sight** (form and color)
- From subtle **water** is born the organ of **taste**
- From subtle **earth** is born the organ of **smell**

"Sense organs," in this case, don't refer to a physical part of the body but rather, the subtle faculties that receive the data we know as sound, touch, sight, taste and smell.

An interesting point to make about the sense organs is their orderly relationship with the five basic elements, so that the first element (space) is recognizable by one sense organ (hearing[7]), the second element (air) is recognizable by two sense organs (hearing and touch), the third element (fire) is recognizable by three sense organs (hearing, touch, and sight), the fourth element (water) is recognizable by four sense organs (hearing, touch, sight and taste), and the last element (earth) is recognizable by five sense organs (hearing, touch, sight, taste, and smell). It's for this reason that the earth element appears more substantial to us than space (which, due to our limited ability to perceive it, appears only as a container for other objects).

The data collected from the sense organs has to go somewhere in order to be useful. So, from the sattva aspect of each of the subtle elements is also born the **inner organ** whose main job is to collect the stimuli from the sense organs and interpret it. The inner organ is four-fold and includes the mind, intellect, ego, and memory. The mind weighs the pros and cons of every situation, and is also associated with emotions and feelings. Deliberate inquiry is the intellect, the deciding faculty. The ego is the I-sense and how one relates to the world. Last is memory, which stores thoughts.

Up until now, we've only discussed the influence of *sattvaguna* on the microcosm. Next, we'll move to *rajoguna* which is responsible for the **five organs of action**.

- From the rajas aspect of **space**, is produced the organ of **speech**
- From the rajas aspect of **air**, the **hands**
- From the rajas aspect of **fire**, the **legs**
- From the rajas aspect of **water**, the **anus**
- From the rajas aspect of **earth**, the **genitals**

The organs of action, like the sense organs, are not physical organs but rather, an aspect of the subtle body that instructs those parts of the body toward action.

In addition, rajoguna produces the **five vital forces** or energy required to operate the body's physiology.

- Respiratory function
- Excretory function
- Circulatory function
- Digestive function
- Reversing function

The reversing function is the physiological emergency actions that rid the body of toxins by means of vomiting, sneezing, tearing, or other ways. It is the body's method of quickly and effectively removing that which doesn't belong in it.[8]

That leaves us with *tamoguna*. Tamoguna is responsible for the creation of the gross elements and in regard to the microcosm, uses the same process as the macrocosm to create the elements and components from which the body is constructed. Thus, sattva and rajas make up the subtle body and tamas makes up the gross body.

The chart below shows how the microcosmic mirrors the macrocosmic.

	Macrocosmic (Totality)	Microcosmic (individual)
Causal Universe/Causal Body	Maya; the seed state; the potential state of creation; the knowledge or blueprint for the manifestation of the universe.	The subconscious; stored tendencies; ignorance; the bliss sheath; associated with the deep sleep state.
Subtle Universe/Subtle Body	The five subtle elements; pure sattva as intelligence.	The internal organ (mind, intellect, memory and ego); the five organs of perception; the five organs of action; the five vital forces; associated with the dream state.
Gross Universe/Gross Body	The five gross elements; a predominance of tamas as inert matter.	The physical body (five gross elements); associated with the waking state.
Consciousness	Consciousness reflected on an unblemished medium (pure sattva); awareness in the form of knower; Identification with all that is (causal, subtle and gross universe).	Consciousness reflected on a dull medium (sattva contaminated by rajas and tamas); awareness in the form of infinitely diverse living beings; identification with the reflecting medium, i.e., the body-mind-sense complex (causal, subtle and gross bodies)

Reflected Consciousness and
Original Consciousness

Comparing the creation of the macrocosm with the creation of the microcosm, we can now see that both have three bodies (gross, subtle, causal) and that the process of creating the three bodies is carried out by the three gunas (rajas, tamas, sattva). The subtle basic elements (space, air, fire, water, earth) combine to make the gross basic elements, which in turn, combine to make objects, sentient beings and the world as we know it. In view of all this, Brahman's only contribution as pure consciousness is its presence. We might compare Brahman to the sun, which shines on the activities of the world but doesn't participate in them.

If we reflect the sun in a mirror, we don't say the mirror is the sun because the mirror is only the reflecting medium. Likewise, the reflection itself is not the sun either. In the same way, the three bodies—which are inert and have no life of their own—are each considered separate reflecting mediums of Brahman's light of consciousness. Thus, the causal body is one reflecting medium, the subtle body is an another, and the gross body is another. The same is true at the macro-level for the causal universe, subtle universe and gross universe.

If we line up all six reflecting mediums (RM) there will be six reflections (RC for reflected consciousness) but only one original source—the "light" (OC for original consciousness). What do each of the reflecting mediums reflect?—original consciousness (God 1; Brahman).

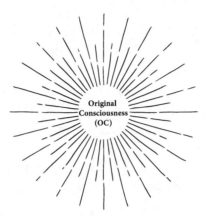

Original
Consciousness
(OC)

MICROCOSM (Individual)	MACROCOSM (Totality)

RC1

RM1

Causal Body

RC4

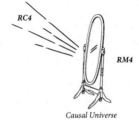

RM4

Causal Universe

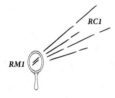

RC2

RM2

Subtle Body

RC5

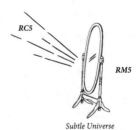

RM5

Subtle Universe

RC3

RM3

Gross Body

RC6

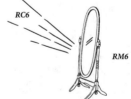

RM6

Gross Universe

Next, we need to consider the quality of the reflecting mediums. A reflecting medium is only as good as its size and ability to reflect. A small dull mirror is not going to reflect as much light as a large shiny one. Unfortunately, for the individual, the mirror is small and dull due to the contamination of rajas and tamas, resulting in our limited knowledge and power. On the other hand, when the light is shone onto unblemished cosmic intelligence (pure sattva), God 2 is given omniscience and the ability to organize and conduct the entire cosmos. This intelligence governs not only the physical laws, but also the psychological and moral laws that apply to all individuals. What about inanimate objects? Matter is inert and doesn't reflect consciousness due to the predominance of tamas. For this reason, matter isn't able to do, think or feel.

However, it's important to keep in mind that the knowledge and powers apparent in God 2 and the individual is only a distortion of original consciousness. One appears to have superior qualities over the other but in reality, both are just original consciousness distorted by a different reflecting medium. As an individual, the key is to not identify with the distorted reflection because that isn't who/what you are. What you are is the light, not the mirror or its reflection. If I look at myself in the mirror and think, "What an ugly face!" I know it's only a distorted version of me and that the outward form of imperfection is due to the reflection, not the real me (original consciousness).

The wise are able to assimilate this knowledge and are not fooled by mere appearances. Ignorance is rooted in us due to maya, which conceals the knowledge of original consciousness reflected in the different mediums (gross, subtle, and causal bodies). Sadly, most of us are living with the belief that we are a distorted version of our true Self. It's as if we were living in a House of Mirrors and had taken our warped refection to be the truth about who we are.

We might be confused by religion when it says God is a

superior being and the individual, a mere dust mote living in an infinite cosmos. Due to our religious upbringing, we might also feel we are a servant to a grand puppet master, one that is forever pulling the strings. However, according to Vedanta, this is only an appearance. We are neither servant, nor is God a master. The point is, our differences are only superficial and incidental. In essence, God and the individual are one. I am both nothing (as an apparent individual) and everything (as the Self). While this might sound like blasphemy, it's one thing to say "I am God, the almighty" and another to say "God and I are one." The former assumes the entity of God as creator, while the latter describes a shared identity. This distinction becomes more clear when it's seen that the individual is in one order of reality and the Self in another.

So, to summarize, within the individual or microcosm there are three related aspects of consciousness: (1) original consciousness which is ever-experienced (2) reflecting mediums, which includes the inert gross, subtle and causal bodies/universes and (3) the reflections, which when combined at the micro-level is the illusory experience of being the body-mind (jiva). The combined body-mind appears to gain consciousness but in reality, is just a reflecting medium and never becomes consciousness itself. Due to maya, we believe we are the reflection (a distorted version of original consciousness), which causes us to suffer and struggle to perfect that which can never be perfected.

Lastly, it's important to note that the macrocosmic (the world) isn't actually a self-creating, self-sustaining, or self-destroying independent entity. Just like the microcosmic (the individual), the world is lifeless and inert without original consciousness. Again, the point of all this is to show that everything originates from God as pure consciousness. Ultimately, the purpose of religion is to "reconnect" (from the Latin word, *religare*) the reflected self or "soul" back to God. If you follow the light all the way back to its source, God as original consciousness is where it will eventually lead you to.

Notes

1. In his book *Indian Mythology: Tales, Symbols, and Rituals from the Heart of the Subcontinent,* author Devdutt Pattanaik writes that from a spiritual perspective, Brahma creates the paradigm of life in order for us to discover our true identity, Vishnu helps us establish stability in life so we can experience a sense of harmony and order, and Shiva is what makes it possible for us to challenge the paradigm, withdraw from it and find our identity outside of it.

2. Campbell, Joseph. *Myths of Light: Eastern Metaphors of the Eternal.* Joseph Campbell Foundation, 2018. p.54.

3. We are made of the stuff of stars, or more accurately, the nuclear ash that resulted from the first stars exploding and leaving behind remnants of their chemical products. Our solar system, including our body, was formed out of such cosmic detritus.

4. According to science, the "Big Crunch" is when dark energy — the mysterious force that's causing the rate of expansion of our universe to speed up over time — diminishes and goes negative, therefore, contracting instead of expanding.

5. Kuhn, Robert Lawrence "Forget Space-Time: Information May Create the Cosmos." *Space.com,* May 23, 2015.

6. While knowledge of a cosmic seed form has existed in India for thousands of years, the concept first appeared in the West in 1927 when a Belgian priest and theoretical physicist named Abbe Georges Lemaitre proposed that the universe begun as a "Cosmic Egg," that is, a high-density state that expanded with explosive force — an idea that would later become the modern Big Bang theory.

7. The logic being that sound apparently travels through space.

8. According to scripture, the reversing function also operates at the time of death, separating the subtle body from the gross body via the crown of the head.

Chapter 4

One Great Order

I will now tell you, Arjuna, the best of the Kurus, my divine glories in keeping with their prominence, because there is no limit to my glories. (Bhagavad Gita, 10.19)

It's not enough that God only provide the blueprints and material for creation. To preserve the creation, there must also be order built into the system. The original meaning of the word "cosmos," as used by Pythagoras in the sixth century, was "order," "harmony" or "beauty." It could be said that all science is really a search for unification and underlying order.[1] This is evident in such discoveries as the link between the motion of the earth and the movement of the moon, the finding that magnetism and electricity are related, and the realization that energy and mass are the same.

We find order in everything from the smallest subatomic particles to entire planetary systems. The sheer magnitude and complexity of the universe's order is far greater than any one person could ever grasp. To do so, you would need to be an expert in every scientific discipline and be able to understand how each one connects, relates and functions with the other (and that's assuming you already know everything there is to know!). As humans, we are good at understanding parts of the universe, but will never be able to understand it in its entirety. With our limited brain power, we simply can never fully comprehend the awesome order that governs and connects all the different elements and forces that make up this apparent reality.

Einstein, once aptly compared us to a child in an immense library who senses there is organization, but still struggles to grasp what they are looking at:

The human mind, no matter how highly trained, cannot grasp the universe. We are in the position of a little child, entering a huge library whose walls are covered to the ceiling with books in many different tongues. The child knows that someone must have written those books. It does not know who or how. It does not understand the languages in which they are written. The child notes a definite plan in the arrangement of the books, a mysterious order, which it does not comprehend, but only dimly suspects. That, it seems to me, is the attitude of the human mind, even the greatest and most cultured, toward God. We see a universe marvelously arranged, obeying certain laws, but we understand the laws only dimly. Our limited minds cannot grasp the mysterious force that sways the constellations.[2]

Order connotes intelligence or the purposeful organization of random elements into something meaningful such as a sequence, pattern or method. However, an orderly universe doesn't mean there is not chaos. Within the framework of order there can exist chaos just like within a game (a form of play based on a set of rules) there is sometimes chaos (e.g., skirmishes between players). But even with a massive cosmic event such as two galaxies colliding, the involved destructive forces must still obey the basic laws and processes of physics. In short, nothing in the universe gets to make its own laws.

Nature might sometimes appear inexplicable (i.e., quantum physics) but it is still always operating within a pre-determined set of principles. Thus, there is chaos found within order but there's never not order. Order and chaos are not a dichotomy. When things do appear random in nature, it's usually not until the cause for their randomness is understood that the underlying order is made obvious.

For example, on the surface, global warming appears to be just a case of "global weirding"—a hiccup in the long history of Earth's climate. But in reality, it's the result of man-made factors contributing to a system that is not unaffected by high concentrations of greenhouse gases. In other words, global warming is not some random event. It's the effect of an order being disrupted. In this case, the order happens to be a highly interconnected, self-regulating system which enables the consistent weather patterns that support life on this planet. In this way, today's extreme weather events might be viewed as the order sending us feedback. And if we continue to ignore the feedback, the order has other self-regulating means that don't necessarily favor the longevity of our species.

Predictability is one aspect of order. Without order, scientists wouldn't be able to make any of their calculations or models. It's because things consistently follow a pattern that we are able to predict certain outcomes (e.g., man-made global warming was predicted decades ago before extreme weather events became the norm). Scientists rely on predictability using mathematical equations to describe the world in ever-finer detail. Both Galileo and Newton regarded the physical laws as God's thoughts, and nature's elegant mathematical form as a display of God's intelligent plan.

If we think about it, it's quite remarkable, peculiar even, that math equations should be able to predict the existence of such things as antimatter, neutrinos and black holes. The reason for this, as Galileo observed, is because mathematics is the language of nature. Humans didn't invent mathematics in order to describe the world, the formulas have always been there waiting to be discovered. This has led more than one scientist to suggest that God is a mathematician. Nobel Prize winning physicist Richard Feynman once said, "Why nature is mathematical is a mystery.... The fact that there are rules at all is a kind of miracle."

In his book *The God Equation*, physicist Michio Kaku marvels at the remarkable beauty, order and simplicity of the universe and the fact that all the known laws of the physical universe can be summed-up on a single sheet of paper. He describes this single sheet of paper as containing Einstein's theory of relativity and the Standard Model[3] (which takes up most of the sheet of paper with its multitude of subatomic particles). Kaku's point is that it's hard not to conclude that a cosmic designer is behind such an elegant design. He makes the admission that everything in physics becomes simpler and more powerful with time, and yet, there are some things beyond even the scope of science.

Order also connotes an object's nature or innate programming. Order is why water is always wet and fire is always hot. At the sentient level, all animals, plants and microbes have an innate programming that indicates what their tasks are and in exactly what way they should be carried out. Everything in the universe is built for a specific function. Even within our own species, we find those who are inclined to do one task, while others are inclined to do another. Society benefits from the different roles individuals play just like the forest benefits from the different roles plants, animals, and microbes, play. Few people choose a particular career path in order to do what's best for the Total, and yet, like an ant colony, we all benefit from a sort of symbiosis so that, for example, as humans, most of us needn't worry about growing our own food or making our own clothes. Thus, order is to be found everywhere, is present in ways we might have not considered, and is not without purpose.

Another Nobel Prize winning physicist, Steven Weinberg, believes that great theoreticians like Paul Dirac and the nineteenth-century physicist James Clerk Maxwell were guided by the aesthetic beauty found in mathematics. So, order is also related to beauty found in the deep underlying principles that govern the world. Physicist, Jim Al-Khalili in his book *The World According to Physics* remarks that this beauty is no less awe-inspiring than a spectacular sunset or a great work of art. He further explains that this beauty doesn't lie in the profundity of the laws of nature but in the deceptively simple explanations from which they come.

Lastly, order suggests rules. You can't have a game without rules and you certainly can't have a cosmos without them either. Universal laws create limitations for what an object or group of objects can or cannot do. In physics, these include such constants as the speed of light, the mass of a proton, or the constant of gravitational attraction. For example, an electron has the same charge whether measured here on earth or in a galaxy billions of light years away. And the charge they have now is the same charge they have had since the beginning of time. It is also widely accepted that certain universal laws cannot ever be violated, such as the law of conservation of energy.

Not only is it evident that there are rules in nature, but also a certain compartmentalizing that allows complex systems to work. This is evident in the organization of the cell with its chemical micro-environments, the human body with its organs, the earth system with its subsystems, and even entire cities in the way they are divided into various functions that include roads, schools, hospitals, police stations, water supply systems, sewage disposal plants, and more. Without order, none of these complex systems would be possible.

Besides governing the material universe and the laws of inert objects, God also governs the field of experience in which individuals play out their lives. For humans, life not only involves the application of physical laws, but psychological and moral laws too. Because of these laws, human beings are not inclined to, for example, ingest certain objects (a physical limitation), expose themselves to situations that cause acute emotional disturbance (a psychological limitation), or carry out actions that make one feel culpable (a moral limitation). This last point is one aspect that clearly differentiates humans from other sentient beings. We are unique in the way that it's difficult for us to ignore the negative psychological repercussions that come from, for example, lying, stealing, or killing. And that's a good thing! Because without having such laws, society would quickly fall into disarray and misery. Therefore, in spite of our species having a long history of violence, it's mostly our nature to follow certain innate rules that help keep us in harmony with each other.

The following is just a small sample of God's great order. What should be obvious from each is a pattern of interconnectedness. No one system is a system unto itself. If we were able to permanently realize the actual connections and relationships that surround and include us, we would live out the rest of our days in constant bliss knowing that we are never alone or detached from everything that surrounds us. Sadly, we walk through life blinded and removed, embraced by a holy great order that we hardly, if ever, stop to notice. So persistent is our delusion.

Physical Order

The universe is full of examples of physical order at all levels, from the uniform distribution of galaxies and stars in the Milky Way (including our own planetary system—the "solar" system), to molecules and atoms (including particles and their subcomponents). But perhaps none is as remarkable and unlikely as the order that makes life possible. Not only do we find great order within our own physical bodies, but an astonishing order outside it that is perfectly fine-tuned to support us and our little blue planet. For example, if the strong force within atoms were just slightly weaker, there would be no element other than hydrogen, let alone any stars or life anywhere. Or if the universe's basic physical constants (e.g., the gravitational constant) were even 1 percent different, the Sun would not exist. That said, everything from the size of the Sun to the influence of the Moon helps makes life possible in an extremely unlikely universe.

And while the universe isn't without its imperfections, one might ask, how would you make it better? Playing on this idea, physicist and author, Paul Davies[4] suggests that while you might be able to do away with black holes and some galaxies, and erasing some small stars and planets, or throwing away a few of the elements, removing electrons would be a big mistake (because chemistry would no longer be possible), getting rid of neutrons would be a disaster (because then, we would only have hydrogen as an element), not to mention that any messing with the fundamental particles or their properties would be extremely fraught with danger. In short, you would be wise to just leave everything alone!

Biological and Ecological Order

Included in the physical order found in our universe is, of course, our beloved home, Earth. Earth has its own vastly interconnected system that supports all living organisms on the planet. Not only are all organisms connected through its ecosystem, they are also connected by being genetically related along evolutionary roots. Charles Darwin referred to this as "the tree of life" — a reference from the Bible which means if we trace life's source, the smaller branches converge into bigger branches all the way down to a single trunk. Within the tree of life some species may be on adjacent smaller branches and therefore, more closely related (such as humans and apes), but we all eventually become "joined" the further we go back in time and down the trunk. This interconnectedness and relatedness isn't just another interesting scientific correlation, it's core to life's success. All of life is bound by a holistic web of connections that we, as a society, at our own detriment, have chosen to remain willfully ignorant of. Not only do we see a web of interdependent connections in the natural world, but in the world of global finance and politics as well (which, it could be argued, now have just as much influence on the planet as the biological systems).

Within the earth system and its subsystems[5] are processes and cycles governed by the law of conservation. Examples of these processes include erosion, evaporation, convection currents, transpiration and photosynthesis. While examples of the cycles include the food chain, the carbon cycle, nitrogen cycle, water cycle, rock cycle and energy cycle. Some systems are more stable than others. A glacier is a relatively unstable system unable to adapt if the temperature in the atmosphere rises above the melting point of ice, while a tree benefits from a more stable system that can adapt to environmental changes such as water shortage by regulating the rate of water loss through its leaves. All subsystems are connected and overlap in such a way that what affects one, affects all. A disruption in one system can result in a cascade of environmental changes in others as that system attempts to return to some form of stability. For example, an atmospheric temperature rise in one region can trigger a whole slew of changes in another including, a change in evaporation and transpiration rates, a change in weather patterns, a change in the salinity of water bodies, and in types and numbers of species and organisms in an effort to restore equilibrium.

Physiological Order

Within each individual organism there must be order and cooperation between its various components in order for it to work in unity. For instance, the body's delivery system of arteries and veins are of little use without a heart to pump blood through them. Similarly, a finely-tuned system of coordination is required for that which makes it possible for the legs to walk or the mouth to chew and swallow food.

Even within cells, life's smallest building block, we marvel at the almost factory-assembly-line sense of specialization and division of labor. It's miraculous to think that all living beings were originally formed from a single cell! The cell, much like a seed, contains the knowledge necessary for transformation. Cells carry information in the form of genes that are used to build, maintain and reproduce other cells. From the humble cell, there is the potential for life to manifest into something as large as a blue whale or an entire forest of giant sequoia redwood. As for the individual, from the simple cell we get tissues, which give rise to organs, which in turn create organ systems which — again, miraculously — form the human organism.

Just within the human body alone, there are several sub-systems including a circulatory system, digestive and excretory systems, an endocrine system, an exocrine system, an immune and lymphatic system, a muscular system, a nervous system, renal and urinary systems, a reproductive system, a respiratory system and a skeletal system all working harmoniously in order to deliver the human experience.

God governs this physiological order by alerting us when we are falling out of it. The pain experienced when not eating or not sleeping, or not fulfilling some other basic physiological need, is in effect, a means for getting us to pay attention and mind the rules. Not only does the physiological order alert us when we're not getting enough of something, but when we're getting too much. Hence, society's problems with such pandemics as obesity, substance abuse, and work-related burn out. The physiological order also guarantees the body's eventual demise, thus making room for new organisms.

Psychological Order

Today, it's more common to hear about psychological *disorder* than psychological order, including anxiety disorder, eating disorder, bipolar disorder, post-traumatic stress disorder and a list of other psychoses too many to mention. While it's possible for animals to be out of psychological order, it's mostly humans, with our unique intellectual capacity, who suffer from one psychoses or another. Your dog or cat doesn't develop an obsession about their physical appearance, hold grudges, feel regret, dwell on thoughts that make them sick, or contemplate suicide. Only humans are uniquely capable of devising their own personal hell. Unlike the physical, biological, ecological and physiological orders, the psychological order is not visible, which makes it harder to manage and achieve a sense of equanimity. Most of us are never taught about psychological order or have the slightest clue what it's supposed to look like, which is unfortunate because it leaves us vulnerable to identifying with destructive emotions that wreak havoc on ourselves and others.

God governs the invisible psychological order much like God governs the physiological order—via pain. Psychological suffering isn't something to ignore or to just learn to live with. Like a broken bone, it's something we should want to mend. Psychological order means there's a limit to what we're able to mentally and emotionally engage with and manage as human beings. Unless you're a psychopath or sociopath, you're not immune to psychological laws (and yet, even the psycho and sociopaths eventually find their limits within God's order). Many soldiers return home from war with post-traumatic stress disorder (PTSD) because while being able to survive the physical wounds of war (even the loss of a limb), they grossly overestimated their capacity to survive the emotional ones. They forgot to figure in the cost of war's psychological *disorder* (something that modern militaries are just now beginning to address).

Cognitive Order

Logic tells us that the laws of physics and how the sense organs interpret them must be the same for all observers. Unless we deliberately cover our eyes and ears, we cannot choose not to see or hear something. Which means not only do the laws of physics show order, but so do our sense organs in the way they decipher sense objects. In other words, the world doesn't just require objects and awareness to function, but a mind that works correlatively with nature so that the world can be perceived and understood. For example, the way some beings perceive color and others don't. Everything we visually see exists in the mind, which receives information and interprets it using rules and calculations that create attributes such as brightness, depth and a sense of time and space. In fact, with some clever neurological engineering you could make everything that has a certain color—let's say red—move, make a noise, make you hungry, or even want to have sex (which is what happens with some birds).

God governs the cognitive order through our ability to interpret information both consciously and unconsciously. This involves the participation of both the subtle and causal bodies. Another name for the microcosmic causal body is the subconscious—that part of us which interprets our environment without requiring focused attention. For example, how we are able to automatically recognize certain objects (e.g., the difference between a fork, knife and spoon) and physical locations (e.g., where you live) with little or no effort. Daniel Kahneman in his book *Thinking, Fast and Slow* describes two orders in which we think. System 1 is defined as fast, intuitive, and automatic, while System 2 is defined as slower, more deliberative, and more logical. Vedanta would recognize System 1 as the causal body and System 2 as the subtle body.

Because of cognitive order, humans are able to communicate with one another, have empathy and work together toward common goals. However, that doesn't mean there is never cognitive disorder. We are emotional beings, which means we are prone to doing certain things out of spite or out of heated passion even when it appears illogical or is against our own best interests. In fact, cognitive disorder is what unscrupulous people use to influence an audience and manipulate them. Their objective is to confuse the mind into interpreting information in a way that allows them to create their own preferred order or reality. Like maya, they are skilled at the art of concealment and projection and know exactly how to push our buttons a certain way so they can get what they want from us. Certain politicians, corporate leaders and media hosts are particularly adept at this. More often than not, the favored tactic for creating cognitive disorder is the use of fear, which takes advantage of our innate tendency to worry about unforeseen danger.

Dharmic Order

The *dharmic* order is the rules of proper conduct. It's the order that allows us to know the difference between what's right and what's wrong. Its guiding principle is "do no harm," and although it should apply to all beings and the environment, it mostly serves to protect human beings from each other. When we follow *dharma* we are not only showing respect for other people, but also preventing future retribution. Honoring the dharmic order and maintaining "good karma" are important because they help ensure a reasonably peaceful life. There will always be some who wish to stir the pot, but most individuals prefer not to be plagued with guilt or fear of retaliation, and because of this, are careful regarding the cause and effect of their actions. When the greater dharmic order is threatened, society begins to break down. Corruption, crime and extreme inequality are the usual signs of disunity and a waning dharmic order. Democracy, in particular, is an inherently moral and dharmic enterprise. It depends on the voluntary moral actions of individuals in order for it to function. An *adharmic* society where leaders and citizens don't take personal responsibility for their actions is doomed to failure.

In the Bhagavad Gita, Arjuna is fighting to restore the dharmic order which has been acutely debased by his villainous cousins. The war, as depicted in the Gita, is what is called a *dharmayuddha* — a righteous war in order to uphold the universal moral laws that keep civilization together and in balance. World War II and the Great Alliance's fight against fascism is an example of a dharmayuddha at a time when the world's dharmic order was put in serious peril.

Dharmic order also represents rules based on roles and responsibilities. Without dharmic order nothing is consistent or predictable, circumstances become unmanageable and chaos ensues. For example, in a society where government leaders don't uphold their promises, where partners and friends are unfaithful to each other, or where sons and daughters act against their parents, uncertainty and instability are certain to transpire. This isn't just church-talk. When the predictable rhythms of nature are absent, society becomes anxious resulting in a negative effect. The fact that many countries are currently witnessing cracks in some of their most valued institutions is a sign that the dharmic order is being threatened.

Total Order

To summarize, whatever we do, wherever we go, we are in God's order. We are never not interacting with God. It's all God—including this body and the mind and how they work. God is not only this body and mind, but the source and totality of all bodies and minds combined (the "cosmic person").

In the Shvetashvatara Upanishad it's written:

His eyes are everywhere, his faces everywhere, his arms everywhere. Everywhere are his feet. He is that which endows beings with arms, birds with feet and wings, and men likewise with feet... (3.3)

God's order includes everything except for the small "me" I believe I am because "me" is an illusion that says I am separate and apart from God's order. It's the wave believing it's separate from the ocean. It's that which has us forget that God's order is what makes even the simplest of things possible. In the conversation with the atheist, the sage reminds us that even with everyday objects, we can see the immense interconnection and order that makes it possible. He tells us to, "Look at everything that had to occur for even a single sheet of paper to manifest — the sun, the water, the tree, the lumberjack, the chainsaw, the truck, the sawmill, the paper factory, the salesperson, the retailer..."

Unlike certain scientists of the past and present, we needn't picture the Total Order as a cold, purposeless universe of random objects and mechanistic forces. Instead, like others, such as Newton, Darwin and Einstein, we can have reverence for the idea of a power or cosmic intelligence behind the universe. We can marvel at how everything just seems to work and how against all odds, life and the human experience persists.

Charles Darwin was originally headed for a career with the Church before he seized the opportunity to spend a nearly five-year scientific adventure aboard HMS Beagle. His wonderment of nature is evident when he writes in *Voyage of the Beagle*:

Among the scenes which are deeply impressed on my mind none exceed in sublimity the primeval forests un-defaced by the hand of man; whether those of Brazil, where the powers of life are predominant, or those of Tierra del Fuego, where death and decay prevail. Both are temples filled with the varied productions of the God of nature. No one can stand in these solitudes unmoved, and not feel that there is more in man than the mere breath of his body.

Notes

1. Originally there was no word for "science." Up until about Newton's time, it was referred to instead as "natural philosophy." The roots of science come from classical antiquity and Greek philosophy which attempted to provide an explanation for the order found in nature.

2. Albert Einstein, in an interview published in *Glimpses of the Great* by George Sylvester Viereck. 1929.

3. The Standard Model of particle physics is the classification of all the known elementary particles, as well as the theory that describes the four known fundamental forces in the universe. It consists of six quarks, six leptons, five known bosons and a postulated sixth, Higgs boson, in addition to the four physical forces: the strong force, weak force, the electromagnetic force, and the gravitational force. However, as author Bill Bryson once noted, most particle physicists have the opinion that the Standard Model lacks elegance and simplicity. Physicist, Leon Lederman in a 1985 PBS documentary said, "We don't really see the creator twiddling twenty knobs to set twenty parameters to create the universe as we know it."

4. Davies, Paul. *The Goldilocks Enigma: Why Is the Universe Just Right for Life?* Mariner Books, 2008. p.85.

5. The Earth's subsystems include the hydrosphere (water), geosphere (interior and surface of Earth), atmosphere (gases), cryosphere (ice) and biosphere (living beings).

Chapter 5

The Field of Experience

In Chapter 3, I compared the individual's relationship to God 2 as the microcosmic. The individual was shown to exist as the five basic elements along with a gross, subtle and causal body. Because God 2 involves creation and creation involves maya, the gunas play a role in the manifestation of the individual. The subtle body and sense organs evolve from sattvaguna, the organs of action and the vital organs evolve from rajoguna, and the physical body evolves from tamoguna. With that brief review, we can now expand on the relationship between God and the individual or, as it's known in Sanskrit, the *jiva*.

God 2 controls maya and maya, in turn, controls the jiva. God 2 is like a spider moving freely on its own web while the jiva constantly gets entangled in it. At the most basic level, a jiva is a subtle body illuminated by consciousness and can be described in two different ways. The first is the impersonal eternal Jiva (capital "J") defined as the archetype,[1] the totality of all individuals, or the "cosmic person." This is what Arjuna is describing in Chapter 11 of the Bhagavad Gita when he says:

> I witness your infinite form, where I see from all sides, countless arms, stomachs, mouths, and eyes. There is no end, no middle, nor beginning to your creation, O Lord of the cosmic form! (11.16)

Vedanta often challenges us by looking at something from different, sometimes changing, points of view. It's for this reason that it can sometimes appear to make contradictory statements.[2] It's similar to looking at a tree from above, from below and through a powerful microscope. From a 10,000-foot view, the tree will appear very small, or because we see only the top, look like something else. From ground level, looking up, the tree may look huge as if it were a world unto itself. However, if we look at the tree using a very powerful instrument (such as a particle accelerator), it will appear to be only atoms and subatomic particles. If we look even closer, one might only view the empty space between the particles and conclude there is no tree! Thus, like science, Vedanta's method often includes us considering a perspective we may not yet be familiar with.

Because the basic qualities of each individual are more or less the same (including the five basic elements, the three bodies, the five sense organs, etc.), we can say phenomenally, there are many individuals but intrinsically, there is only one. Thus, in actuality there is only one eternal Jiva appearing as many apparently unique individuals. If the opposite were true and individuals were all intrinsically dissimilar, scripture would have no value because everybody's nature would be different and we would all be left to our own devices in order to find a way through life (which, ironically, is what most people believe). That not being the case, we might ask where do all these shared basic universal qualities come from? Answer: they come out of maya and exist until the end of the creation cycle when they return to their unmanifest state. So, as individuals, we might appear different, but we mostly share all the same attributes. As the eternal Jiva, we are all the "son of God."

In contrast, the non-eternal jiva (small "j") is the separate, personal individual we believe ourselves to be. It is pure consciousness conditioned by the body-mind on account of ignorance (*avidya*).[3] Under the spell of maya it believes, "I am the doer,[4] thinker, perceiver, and knower." However, this is wrong because it is God that does, thinks, perceives, and knows through the instrument. Similarly, the jiva's I-sense misconstrues its relationship with consciousness thinking it is part of the body-mind. But we know this can't be true either because the doer is not always present, for example, during deep sleep when all identification with being a person is paused. So, consciousness can only belong to God 1 and the doer can only belong to God 2. Where does that leave "me"? "Me" is just a story with no inherent reality—at best, a persistent illusion.

The Three Orders of Reality

The Field of Experience is the arena in which jivas play out the game of life working for results. To begin to define the Field of Experience, it helps to define the three orders of reality that make up the jiva's experience, including absolute reality, objective reality and subjective reality.

Absolute reality has already been defined in multiple ways as God 1, satya, Brahman, and original consciousness (OC). Absolute reality is defined as that which cannot be negated. It is the realm of pure, unmodified, limitless, attributeless, ordinary, ever-present, all-pervasive, non-dual consciousness.

Next, is objective or transactional reality. This is God 2 or Brahman with attributes (saguna Brahman). Objective reality is maya, God's creation, and is the physical reality that together, we all experience every day. Objective reality is governed by universal order and a fixed set of laws.

Last is subjective reality. This is the individual's personal interpretation of the world based on their likes and dislikes, and *vasanas*—stored tendencies held in the causal body. Subjective reality is sometimes called *jiva-shrishti* or "the individual's creation" as opposed to *Ishvara-shrishti* or "God's creation" (objective reality). Each of us walks around ensconced in a bubble of our own making. Inside the bubble is our unique interpretation of the world. Subjective reality takes over when we dream, fantasize or imagine. Fears, projections and mistaken notions all fall under subjective reality.

The power of subjective reality is traditionally shown using the metaphor of the snake and the rope. The story goes that a traveler enters a village at dusk—the time of day when there's a mixture of light and dark. Upon approaching a well, the parched and weary traveler is startled to find a coiled snake lying next to it with its head raised, poised to strike. As he carefully and slowly begins to step away from the menacing snake, a villager passes by with a lantern revealing the "snake" to be just a neatly coiled rope lying next to a bucket. Both relieved and somewhat amused by his misapprehension, the traveler continues his journey with confidence. This analogy is an example of the mind's ability to construct its own reality. The mind is constantly constructing the world in ways we are sometimes unconscious of, which is why knowledge and discrimination (identifying what's real and what's not) are paramount.

The Three States of Experience

Now that we've outlined the three realities that shape the jiva's experience, we can discuss the three roles or states it experiences. Scripture says the eternal Jiva plays three roles as waker (the extroverted state), dreamer (the introverted state) and sleeper (the bliss sheath).

In the extroverted waking state, Jiva is hypnotized by maya and chases and consumes various experiences. Scripture describes the waker as "the one with the thirteen mouths," which refers to the five sense instruments, five sense organs, the mind, intellect, and ego. It is said that the "physical body consumes matter, the mind constantly chews emotion, the intellect eats ideas, and the ego gobbles any experience it believes will make it feel whole, adequate and complete."[5] Jiva, as waker, identifies with objects believing they hold the key to their lasting fulfillment and satisfaction. The waking state is often associated with the gross body due to its interaction with physical objects.

Next, is the dreamer, dubbed "the shining one" due to awareness, via the subtle body, illumining the dream state without the involvement of any external objects. In the dream state the subtle body is turned inward in the direction of the causal body where it experiences vasanas stored from past experiences. Another way to understand a vasana is as an impression left in the subconscious in the form of a like or dislike. Vasanas manifest in the dream state like patchwork, expressing themselves in often creative and incoherent ways. The reason why dreams are often unintelligible is because the intellect isn't present to organize and make sense of them. Nevertheless, to the dreamer the dream state appears just as real as the waking state. The dream state is associated with the subtle body due to its role in illumining internal objects.

Lastly, the sleep state is associated with the macrocosmic causal body. It's interesting to note that the word for "sleeper" in Sanskrit is *prajna*, meaning "almost enlightened." The sleeper is almost enlightened because while experiencing the limitlessness or bliss of consciousness, it lacks knowledge of what it is experiencing. This is because the subtle body is absent during deep sleep and unable to process any information. Another way to describe prajna is consciousness identifying with the macrocosmic causal body.

The deep sleep state is dominated by tamoguna (maya's concealing power). During the deep sleep state, there is no I-sense because only the gross body is present. With the chatter of the mind and the vasanas put to rest, there is only consciousness experiencing its own nature. It's for this reason that the deep sleep state is also referred to as the bliss sheath, because it provides Jiva respite from the restless mind (hence, our fondness for sleep).

The teaching of the three states isn't complete without mentioning that which is constant during all three states. Upon further analysis, we can see that in order for the waker to become a dreamer, the waker must disappear; and in order for the dreamer to become a deep-sleeper, the dreamer must disappear;

and in order for the deep-sleeper to become a waker, the deep-sleeper must disappear. The only invariable and ever-present factor is the "knower" of all three states—consciousness. Once again, we find that only consciousness can be real, because Jiva is always changing from one state to the next.

A World of Opposites

Before revealing more about the nature of Jiva, we should describe the nature of the Field, itself. The Field of Experience is created in a particular way so that every attribute has a corresponding opposite, and in a way so that one can't exist without the other. For example, you can't have hot without cold, sweet without sour, or hard without soft. If this duality didn't exist, we wouldn't have a world. This applies to the psychological world as well. Ironically, due to ignorance, Jiva constantly seeks pleasure and runs away from pain without realizing that it can't have pleasure without some pain (and vice versa).

The ancient Chinese yin-yang symbol visually sums up the concept of dualism and a world that is complementary, interconnected and interdependent. The dots signify there is a bit of the other in each opposite. For example, every pleasure carries with it a little pain (e.g., the knowledge that the pleasure will end), and every pain carries with it a little pleasure (e.g., the knowledge that the pain will end). Purity doesn't exist in duality, which means the world can never be perfect and that life without some difficulty is impossible.

This realization might cause one to come to the conclusion that life is a zero-sum and that due to constant changing forces, perfect worldly satisfaction can only be achieved briefly, if at all.[6] In maya's playground, there's an up for every down and a down for every up. As jivas, we suffer because we are unwilling to accept this reality. We instead prefer to go through life believing that our vision of perfection exists out there somewhere and that all we need to do is choose the right career, find the right partner, move to the right country, etc. As a result, our quest for worldly happiness knows no boundaries. The word for this is "samsara," which in many ways represents life's treadmill.

However, it's not only the concept of pairs of opposites that is hard for the jiva to accept. There is also impermanence and the fact that all objects are bound to change (duality's signature attribute). Buddhism states that all objects are ultimately impermanent, unsatisfactory, and empty of substance. The Buddha's main point was that we suffer because we insist on trying to grasp that which cannot be held onto. It's only by the power of maya that we believe certain objects to be reliable independent entities and a permanent source of happiness.

Vedanta describes the impermanent and unreliable nature of objects as being the result of the gunas, which are powers that create not only the "outer world" but our inner one as well. For Jiva, each of the gunas has its own function. Sattva is responsible for the thinking, knowing and perceiving functions; rajas is responsible for the doing and projecting functions; and tamas is ignorance (although, rajas also contributes to ignorance with its ability to project the false). Tamas is responsible for the concealment that causes individuals to doubt and have erroneous knowledge. It does this by clouding the mind and hiding the truth. Both rajas and tamas create our likes and dislikes.

Similar to yin and yang is the concept of the gunas which are constantly flowing through all of nature. This symbol suggests not only the constant movement of the gunas but also shows consciousness (center) as the unmoving substrate.that supports them. Colors may also be assigned to each guna with white representing coolness or clarity (sattva), red representing heat or passion (rajas), and black representing opaqueness or ignorance (tamas). Where one guna begins to taper off, another gains predominance.

The three forces also have the psychological effect of influencing our mental state on a moment-by-moment basis. A mind that is sattvic is focused and balanced, a mind that is rajasic is energized and motivated, while a mind that is tamasic is dull and lethargic. Throughout the day, the gunas fluctuate so that you might feel tamasic one moment, rajasic the next, and sattvic the next. Each guna has a purpose. For example, the jiva needs rajas to get out of bed in the morning, sattva to focus on its work tasks, and tamas to wind down and fall asleep at the end of the day.

Furthermore, an individual's temperament, or jiva-type, is based on his or her guna makeup. For instance, the ideal guna composition for spiritual success in order of predominance would be sattva-rajas-tamas. Those who study Vedanta tend to be predominantly sattvic, which means they are predisposed to pursuing the truth. On the other hand, a predominance of rajas followed by sattva and tamas (rajas-sattva-tamas) is what many leaders exhibit. They bring energy, motivation and clarity together in order to help solve problems and provide direction. Lastly, a jiva with a predominance of tamas constitutes those individuals who are mostly looking for an easy way to get through life, whether it be through menial work or by being small-time criminals. The gunas can also change with the different stages of life. As teenagers spoiled by modern life's many conveniences, we might be tamasic. It's not until we enter the competitive workforce that we become rajasic. Later in life, with our duties completed and our ambitions discarded, we might begin to stop to smell the roses and take on a more sattvic nature.

There's a story told by Swami Nikhilananda in his book *Self-Knowledge (Atmabodha)*[7] that puts the three gunas in perspective and shows how they relate to spiritual attainment. In the story, the three gunas are portrayed as three highway robbers who ambush a lonely traveler lost in the woods. The first robber, tamas, lets his intentions be known that he wants to destroy the man, but rajas, the second robber, persuades the other two that they should instead just bind his hands and feet and take all his belongings. The three leave but after some time sattva's conscience ways heavy and he returns to free the man and accompany him on the path that leads to home. Because sattva is a robber and fearful of the police, he eventually takes leave of the traveler and lets him finish his journey alone. To sum it up: tamas wants to destroy the traveler, rajas binds him to the world and takes his spiritual treasures, and sattva sets him on the path to freedom. For the spiritual aspirant, tamas is to be defeated by rajas, and rajas by sattva. But in the end, even sattva must be given up if freedom is what the aspirant is after, because the truth is only found beyond the three gunas.

The gunas are a fascinating topic that merit much discussion, especially in regard to learning how to manage them in order to maintain a healthy and balanced lifestyle. But for now, the important take-away is that the forces that influence our outer world are the same forces that influence our inner one. It's all impersonal, which is why the wise don't identify with the gunas, choosing instead, to identify with that which is constant and unchanging—the Self.

The Karma Matrix

The verb-root of *karma* is *kr*, meaning "to act, do, make." Therefore, the actual definition of *karma* is "action," which is often used in the context of samsara (the endless cycle of birth and death as a result of ignorance). Karma theory states that because of action that creates vasanas and the belief "I am the doer," beings are propelled endlessly from one life to another until the knowledge "I am the Self" is firmly established. The cessation of the cycle of birth and death is a result of the cause of rebirth no longer being present (the cause being ignorance regarding one's true essence). Because there is no longer any cause, there can be no effect. Thus, the actualization of Self-knowledge is equivalent to liberation from samsara.

However, *karma* can also refer to the effect of my actions and the accumulation of merit. For example, most people are familiar with the concept of having good or bad karma. In the "karma matrix," the jiva is the apparent doer (the initiator of action) and God 2 is the giver of the results of action. The jiva is impelled to act due to its vasanas and the impersonal gunas. Samsara is referred to as a cycle because there is no beginning or end. A vasana (tendency) gives rise to a desire (for an object), which impels an action (karma), which reinforces the vasana, which then, creates another desire, and so on (see below).

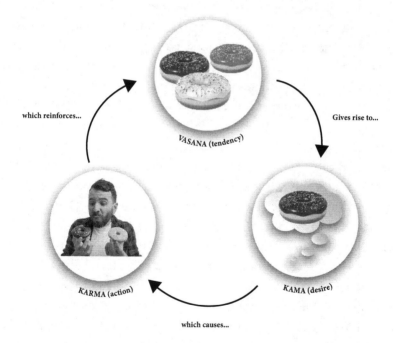

The jiva likes to believe it's in charge of the results of its actions and that it's responsible for manufacturing success—and to a degree, this is true. If it weren't, we wouldn't be able to accomplish anything because we wouldn't be able to rely on even the simplest of actions in order to obtain our desired result. For example, if I'm thirsty, I know that by drinking water the thirst will dissipate. It might not dissipate completely, but it will lessen. Thus, I know I can rely on the action of drinking to remove thirst. However, where it gets tricky is when there are multiple unknowns that are outside my control.

For example, a budding entrepreneur might believe the catchphrase, "build it and they will come," thinking that if only given the opportunity to build the product or service he envisions, customers will spontaneously appear and revenue will start to pour in. Well, maybe it will and maybe it won't! A lot goes into making a successful business including investors, design, engineering, marketing, partnerships, team-building, customer support, location, timing, not to mention luck! Also, as often is the case, actions put out in the Field create long-term unseen effects. Nobody can completely know how the Field is going to respond at any given moment due to its intricate relationships and all the forces at play. This is also why predicting the future is a fool's run, because nobody can ever fully grasp all the unseen dynamics involved (e.g., nobody predicted the internet and the immense global impact it would have). So, the jiva is responsible for its actions, but not the results of its actions. The results are up to the Field (God).

Sometimes the results are immediate (e.g., I just ate and now I'm full), and sometimes the effect of the cause is delayed (e.g., I said something I shouldn't have and now I must await the consequences). You can't stop an arrow mid-flight. Even the enlightened are not immune to the residue of previous acts they must experience. Once karma is put in motion, there is no guarantee when or how it will play out for the jiva. The karma of a deed committed today may take several months or years to manifest. It's for this reason that the wise are careful and selective regarding their actions.

If you want to collect the sweet fruit of karma, you must learn to carefully cultivate your actions like seeds. This isn't some secret business formula for success but mostly just common sense and being mindful of the effect of your actions. People are often disappointed that the bad guys seem to always escape culpability, but nobody is outside the law of karma. Not only are the results of their actions eventually delivered to them, but also to their friends and family who have been stained through association and their decision to jump on their reality-bending bandwagon. The message is: rub against God and God rubs back!

Karma is like having a savings account. Going through life, the jiva accrues both good and bad karma. If their actions are dharmic, they will accrue good karma and reap the fruits. If their actions are adharmic, they will accrue bad karma and suffer the effects. In Vedic cosmology, karma either propels us toward a good future life where our needs are met (including a better opportunity for spiritual growth), or a bad future where instead we're given the opportunity to exhaust our brutish tendencies as animals, insects or other lower beings. But the point isn't to work toward a better next life, but instead, to understand that in order to live a reasonably peaceful life here and now, one should follow dharma. Those who are happiest, consciously or unconsciously, align themselves with God's order. They recognize that this is a lawful and holy universe and have the attitude that while the Field may not always give them what they want, it always gives them what they need. In short, dharma and karma are the two ways God governs the Field of Experience and directs us toward eventual liberation.

The Needs of the Total Come First
It shouldn't go without mention that God always does what's in the best interest of the Total. On the surface, this may sound like a belief or more talk of Big Daddy. But it should be obvious that no one person is an island and that life works best for everyone when there is unity and cooperation. As a society, we most often find conflict when the basic needs of one group is severely ignored by another. In other words, we are in harmony with

God when the needs of everyone are considered, and we are out of harmony when a minority decides their own "needs" take precedent over another's.

God's way of supporting the needs of the Total is not always pretty. Sometimes, destruction, war, famine or disease are necessary to return to a state of equilibrium or bring renewal to a system that has run rampant or become excessively corrupt. Such "adjustments" may be seen as part of God's great order. This in no way justifies xenophobia, sexism, slavery, ethnic cleansing or all the other forms of oppression that humans like to use against each other (we are all part of God's Total). It simply means God doesn't play favorites. God doesn't cater to individuals with selfish desires because their desires are based on ignorance and the belief that they are separate entities apart from the Total. God always does what's best for the Total, including what's best for the environment. The fact that we are now experiencing certain global crises tied to our misuse of the biosphere is a measurement of our hubris and alienation from God. In short, we have lost the fundamental understanding that we are part of something greater. We have turned actual freedom into "my freedoms," revealing just how far off the path we've veered.

The Question of Free Will

All this talk of impersonal forces controlling the jiva and the rules set by God might have you wondering if free will actually exists. To summarize what we've covered so far: As a jiva, I have certain vasanas (tendencies) that define my actions and temperament. My vasanas are formed by my likes and dislikes, which are colored by the gunas. The gunas (in the form of the senses) are compelled by the gunas (in the form of sense objects). A vasana creates a desire, which results in action, which further reinforces the vasana, creating another desire, and so on, resulting in an endless cycle of cause and effect. What was the original cause? It's a chicken-and-egg conundrum. Which came first, the desire or the action? And most important, did I really create the desire or action or is it all just the impersonal gunas? Lastly, where's the doer in all this?

Let's say I have developed a sugar vasana and now have a "sweet tooth." At what moment did I decide I should like sugar? I don't recall ever deciding to like sugar. If I were able to decide to like sugar that would mean I could decide to not like sugar, especially if my liking sugar too much resulted in serious health issues.

To better illustrate the point, let's say I give a baby a lollipop. The baby has never had a lollipop before but when, as the result of the sugar in the lollipop, the pleasure-inducing chemical dopamine is released, a strong liking for lollipops manifests. The strong liking leaves an impression (vasana) and the effect is that the next time the baby sees a lollipop, there is an intense wanting (desire) and it begins to cry (action) until someone gives the baby a lollipop. After some time and more experience with sugar, this creates a tendency for the baby to want anything that is sweet (reinforcing the sugar vasana), making it harder to please the baby with anything that's not sugar (and break the karmic cycle that began with me giving the baby a lollipop). Is it the baby's fault that the sugar from the lollipop triggers the neurotransmitter dopamine in the brain, causing an irresistible rush of pleasure? Is it the baby's fault that this experience leaves a deeply rooted impression, therefore creating a vasana for all things sweet?

With this knowledge, we can begin to see the mechanics of how desire and action work, and wonder who, exactly, is in charge—the jiva or the vasana? Who, or more appropriately, *what* is doing my desires? It's no wonder that addiction is such a common problem among us. Technology has brought us so much efficiency with everything now available "on demand," but it has also created a much stronger desire-trap for us to get caught in. The easier it becomes to satisfy our every desire, the more we reinforce our vasanas, and the harder it gets to pry ourselves away from binding objects—like sugar!

When considering the topic of free will, not only must we look at the karma principle, but the dharma one too. As discussed in the previous chapter on God's order, there are certain limitations built into the Field that indicate what we can and cannot do as individuals. Individuals have contributory free will but not causative free will. The former is about making choices on the actions one takes. The latter is about karma, for which nothing can be done. Karma is like an arrow released from a bow—it can't be stopped mid-flight. There are also physical, psychological and moral guard rails put in place to help make sure we don't just swerve off the road. The laws determine which actions will be rewarded and which ones will be punished (via felt physical or psychological pain).

Scientists like to coldly remind us that from a material perspective, we are nothing but self-sustaining, chemical and physical machines, constructed around information-encoding polymers, produced through evolution by natural selection. Which might make you wonder if we are nothing more than organic robots programmed by the hand of God.

Einstein, who was a fan of the nineteenth-century philosopher, Arthur Schopenhauer, said:

I do not believe in free will. Schopenhauer's words: 'Man can do what he wants, but he cannot will what he wills,' accompany me in all situations throughout my life and reconcile me with the actions of others, even if they are rather painful to me. This awareness of the lack of free will keeps me from taking myself and my fellow men too seriously as acting and deciding individuals, and from losing my temper.[8]

Most likely, Schopenhaur, who was familiar with the Upanishads,[9] drew inspiration from the Kena Upanishad which asks in its opening verse:

> By whose will directed does the mind light upon its object? At whose command does one's life-force proceed to function? At whose volition do men utter speech? What is this intelligence that directs the eyes and ears?

Thus, if we are not willing ourselves to will, then what is? What kind of strange conspiracy is this? And yet as an individual, it *feels* like I am making choices, because apart from any serious health issue or major global event, I have relative control of my circumstances.

So, do I have choice or don't I?

Yes and no. It all comes down to where you're standing. From the jiva's perspective, I am an independent entity with a self-conscious mind capable of carrying out actions. Unlike animals which only operate based on their innate programming, I can reflect on my actions and therefore, have a sense of doership. I don't always make the most appropriate choice but even if I don't, I'm able to make a correction and learn from my experience. Not only that, but I am also able to recondition certain aspects of myself so that I needn't any longer suffer from making the same wrong choices. For example, as a jiva, I can still choose to manage the gunas and cultivate a sattvic demeanor. God may be responsible for the results, but I choose my actions. Even the Gita recommends that "one should lift oneself by oneself" (6.5) and make oneself a friend through control of one's mind and actions. This outlook is important because without it, what's the point of trying to better oneself or ever pursue enlightenment?

As sentient beings, we needn't just roll over and accept our suffering. We should each make a sincere effort to be free of it, and that means managing our vasanas and the gunas. Furthermore, we needn't say "yes" to everything God sends our way, such as undesirable thoughts and emotions. With some work, we can recondition the causal body to form new, healthier patterns and stop the mind from continuously getting stuck in its same old entrenched behaviors.

However, from the macrocosmic view, there is no free will. The Field of Experience is like a big video game where you can only make the moves already programmed in the system. Life is God's game that God plays with itself. God knows exactly what is going to happen today, this month, next year, and for all of eternity. Even wanting enlightenment is God—it's God wanting to return to its natural, blissful state. From God's point of view, there is no free will because everything, right down to subatomic particles, is created and governed by God. It's all impersonal. Not only are we governed by God's laws and conditioned by vasanas, but the gunas influence everything, including our thoughts and feelings. Furthermore, who chooses to be ignorant and suffer as a result? In the end, all vasanas belong to God. The body-mind-sense complex is only a vehicle for their expression.

And so, it appears we are nothing but dream characters in God's dream. For some, this might be distressing until you remember that our essence and God's essence are the same. In other words, whether I view myself as a game piece or not, it doesn't much matter once I identify with the Self. The gunas can come and go and my vasanas can grow or wither. Either way, it's not me. Which means I don't need to take "me" or any of the perceived "others" so seriously. It's all mithya—the illusory expression of impersonal forces.

The conclusion, then, is I am not the doer—which is okay because I am the Self, that which encompasses everything. Why confine my identity to the belief that I'm the limited and doer when I can instead identify with all that is? So, what initially sounds like a very bad deal (I'm not the "me" I thought I was), is a very good one because I'm all existence! This alleviates a multitude of psychological problems associated with the dreadful feeling that, as individuals, we are like an autumn leaf blown hopelessly here and there by a cosmic leaf blower indifferent to our struggle. Thus, upon further analysis we find that the concept of free will is moot for those with Self-knowledge. The doer belongs to God. As for "I"? I am the Self.

Theories about Jiva

The question might arise, if God is everything and omniscient and omnipotent, then why this apparent game of hide-and-seek? Why the needless suffering, seeking, finding and eventual liberation for the jiva?

While it's not possible to demonstrate absolute proof of any motive for the Game of Life, we can speculate on why God, as the jiva, forgets its nature. We know via the teaching of the five sheaths that each sheath has the effect of concealing the truth about who we are. The seeker is first taught to see that the body is not who they are and then, in sequential order, that their physiology, mind, intellect, ego and subconscious (bliss sheath) aren't who they are either. Each sheath obscures the truth of the Self so that we erroneously identify with that which we aren't. So, the **first theory** is that the jiva forgets its nature due to pure consciousness being "covered" by the five sheaths.[10]

Vedanta uses the term *upadhi* to describe a limiting adjunct, which is a fancy way of describing an object that makes something appear other than it is. This was discussed in Chapter 2 using the analogy of the red bottle and how water appears to change color when poured into it. Another example is how the sun reflected in water might appear still or to be moving depending on the condition of the water. Similarly, consciousness, when reflected in the intellect sheath (the sheath responsible for knowledge), becomes endowed with its characteristics. The five sheaths, the subtle body, and reflected consciousness are all synonyms for the eternal Jiva. All are a distortion of original consciousness — our true essence. Thus, the **second theory** is that the jiva forgets its nature due to pure consciousness taking on the qualities of the reflecting medium (the body-mind). This mostly occurs due to the proximity of the body-mind which aids in creating the illusion of "me."

In the first two theories, the jiva's identity with the objective world is so complete that it requires a conscious effort in order to regain it. There is a story told about a group of ten men crossing a river that illustrates this point. Upon making it to the other side, the leader decides to count the men in order to ensure everyone made it across safely. To his dismay, the leader discovers they are only nine. His error, of course, was that he forgot to count himself! In a similar way, the jiva identifies with the body, vital forces, senses, mind, intellect and ego, but loses sight of the Self.

As a **third theory**, we might say that from a cosmological perspective, the jiva is simply Brahman under the influence of maya dreaming that it is a human, animal, plant or other animate object. The jiva's mistake, then, is that it takes itself and the dream to be real. God, in short, is dreaming that it is every sentient being in the universe all at once!

These are all legitimate theories and philosophically, fun to speculate. Unfortunately, why ignorance exists at all will have to remain a mystery. If it helps, one might believe it's all part of the game. In the end, we can only wonder in awe at it all.

Notes

1. The word "archetype" comes from Latin via the Greek word *arkhetupon*, meaning "something molded first as a model."

2. Vedanta uses a teaching method called *adhyaropa-apavada* or "temporary acceptance" that introduces certain teachings provisionally as a means to a more subtle truth. For example, Vedanta teaches that God 1 and God 2 operate in two different orders of reality (satya and mithya). But if that were the case, reality wouldn't be non-dual! However, this teaching is only meant to be temporary. Later, Vedanta

shows that God 2 is God 1, just like the pot is really just clay. Thus, what begins and appears as two (*dvaita*), is shown in the end to be just one (*advaita*).

3. Human beings don't have a monopoly on embodied consciousness. According to Vedanta a jiva can also be an animal, plant, microbe or other being, including those we might not have learned about yet. The difference between a human jiva and another kind of jiva is that a human jiva has a more developed subtle body which includes an intellect. Nevertheless, there are plenty of examples of animals strategizing and even displaying human-like emotional qualities. Even plants have a very rudimentary subtle body that makes them aware from which direction the light is.

4. The jiva is often referred to as the "doer/enjoyer" because it does actions to enjoy the results.

5. Attributed to Vedanta teacher James Swartz.

6. Stanford University psychiatrist Anna Lembke in her book *Dopamine Nation* describes how every pleasure exacts a price in the form of pain and is the reason why addiction eventually intensifies pain while lowering the threshold for pleasure. From this perspective, life seems to push us toward what Buddhism refers to as the middle way—that is, finding middle-ground between extreme self-indulgence and extreme austerity.

7. Nikhilananda, Swami. *Self-Knowledge (Atmabodha)*. Ramakrishna-Vivekananda Center, 1970. p.54.

8. From *My Credo* (1932). Read by Einstein for a recording by the German League of Human Rights.

9. Schopenhauer once remarked that the Upanishads "have been the solace of my life and will be that of my death."

10. Pure consciousness can never actually be covered, it's only our thoughts which make it so, which is why knowledge is paramount to gaining liberation.

Chapter 6

Devotion

Swami Nikhilananda writes in his book *Self-Knowledge* (*Atmabodha*)[1]:

A true philosopher has something of the spirit of awe, adoration, and reverence cherished by a religious person; and a truly religious person is not without the intellectual understanding and insight which are the chief characteristics of a philosopher.

Nikhilananda suggests that religion and knowledge are incomplete without each other and that "The goal of philosophy may be Truth, and the goal of religion, God; but in the final experience God and Truth are one and the same reality."

Religion satisfies the heart, while Self-knowledge satisfies the intellect. Together, they lead the devotee toward liberation. Nikhilananda further elaborates, "Religion supplies the aspirant with feeling or passion, and philosophy prevents him from wandering into dark alleys or up dead ends." One provides the fuel to focus one's life on a higher objective (i.e., union with God), while the other keeps his or her feet firmly planted in reality without veering into magical thinking.

In the traditional sense, religion is associated with devotional practices, ritual, and belief in a higher entity. Spirituality[2], on the other hand, in its truest form, is directed toward personal growth, living responsibly, and learning and contemplating the nature of existence. Both have their place and can even be practiced together. However, spirituality is generally for mature individuals who see the limitations of happiness found in the material world. That said, if Self-knowledge is spirituality, it's spirituality at the highest order.

Many in the West have acquired a particular disgust for religion, accusing it of dogmatism, superstition, and naiveté, among other things. Their frustration is not unfounded. However, for those firmly against religion, their only proposed solution is often to throw the baby out with the bath water. In its place, they kneel at the altar of science, which appeals to the needs of reason and the intellect, but mostly ignores the heartfelt emotional requirements of individuals seeking a means to deal with life's many ups and downs. In other words, we shouldn't be too eager to dismiss religion. Whether we choose to admit it or not, an integral part of being human is not only seeing the world through the mind, but feeling it through the heart.

Religious ritual is also important to many devotees for its affirmation of belief and community. While psychologists may now occupy the role as the new high priests of society, their practice lacks a sense of the sacred and community that religion offers. There is something special about worshiping together that is not easily replaced by an office visit. In modern times, we seem to have done away with the sacred and communal. Instead, our desire for community has moved to social media, where it stews in outrage, conspiracy theories and rampant consumerism.

As humans, we also recognize the importance of having certain values and expressing those values with other like-minded individuals. Otherwise, we run the risk of learning values from popular culture and the media (which in the end is mostly just interested in telling you whatever you want in order to turn a profit). People need structure in their life and a means to navigate it properly. Religion provides this at a basic level to people of all ages.

Vedanta teacher and author James Swartz defines a devotee as "someone who recognizes his or her dependence on God and either wants God's stuff, knowledge of God or non-separation from God."[3] Sincere people approach religion for many reasons.

They may be seeking not only virtue, but comfort, healing, a sense of peace, release from the ambivalence of nature, or simply a means to converse with the mystery. They approach it at different levels of maturity and with different capacities for understanding. Some don't have the fascination with or curiosity to pursue God-knowledge. They still believe the world or the afterlife is capable of providing real happiness. They like to keep their spiritual aspirations at a very basic level, preferably one that is based on fulfilling their personal desires. They are often satisfied having a simple child-parent relationship with God. For them, God is protector and the divine giver of wishes. Such devotees learn best through parables that include only slivers of the truth. Because such individuals tend to be insecure, they have no interest in anything that challenges the status quo or their sense of individuality. They may also see religion as an integral part of their family and culture, and are quite fine being told what to believe. In fact, they would feel irreverent for ever questioning it. Religion to them is like being on a raft in the middle of the ocean—something never to question or to tamper with.

However, the downside of religion is that it tends to satisfy the devotee only at an emotional level. A child worships out of fear, obedience and attachment. Religion is sometimes criticized as "kindergarten spirituality" where even veteran devotees are still taught "Jesus loves you." Mostly this is due to a lack of God-knowledge at the highest levels by those who have little more to offer other than allegories and aesthetics, rather than an actual roadmap to spiritual achievement and independence. But even at the emotional level, religion doesn't cover many of the important fundamental human issues, including topics such as sense-control and management of binding likes and dislikes (the cause of most of our problems).

As humans, our intellect is our most precious gift. To eliminate it from our relationship with God ignores our innate need to make sense of the world and understand who we are, which is what many religions do when they tell you to "just have faith." Religion expects its followers to abandon logic and the need to explain improbable events. Moving from religion to spirituality takes courage for most aspirants, because it requires that the aspirant temporarily subdue their beliefs in order to learn something different, maybe even counter-intuitive. Most religious followers have a difficult time imagining God to be anything other than a personal God—and that's fine. The point isn't to judge another's devotion or put them on a graded scale. People approach God at different levels. In the Gita, Krishna recognizes and encourages devotees of all stripes, not just those pursuing Self-knowledge.

Vedanta recognizes the value of religion as an important initial step in the process toward liberation and encourages practices that nurture one's relationship with God. However, it views religion as being dualistic due to its marked separation between the devotee and God. This doesn't mean religion is wrong, just that once you reach a certain spiritual level, religion is limiting and can be an impediment to gaining *moksha* (ultimate freedom/union with God).

The differences between non-dualistic devotion and dualistic devotion are outlined as follows:

God 1 Devotees	God 2 Devotees
See God as...	*See God as...*
Ineffable	Lord of the universe
Indefinable	Creator
Eternal	Sustainer
Formless	Destroyer
Actionless	Benefactor
Attributeless	Omniscient and omnipresent
Immutable	Universal form
Absolute	Source and origin of all beings

In summary, religion has an important role to play providing us with emotional support, a moral foundation, and a starting point for our spiritual journey. But to remove the intellect and limit it to just ritual and prayer only leads us "wandering into dark alleys or up dead ends." We should aspire to approach God not only through the heart, but through the mind as well so that devotion will eventually lead to knowledge. Questions from a devotee that challenge their faith should be welcomed, not shunned or glossed over, because those questions are where the journey to God-knowledge and actual freedom begins.

The following has been adapted from my book *The Wisdom Teachings of the Bhagavad Gita*. As already suggested, there are different kinds of devotees as well as different stages of devotion. Both topics are extensively covered in the Gita and are interesting in the way they suggest a method leading up to Self-actualization and union with God. According to karma theory, we all eventually reach the end-goal (moksha) by moving through numerous lives and the various stages of devotion, as well as, exhausting our karma and earning the grace necessary to take us over the finish line. In other words, Vedanta says it's not a question of whether or not you're on your way to liberation—we all are on our way. We're all devotees whether we know it or not, because everything is given to us and we are all completely dependent on God as benefactor. Furthermore, we are all consciously or unconsciously seeking the same goal—freedom. The only difference being that most of us are painfully seeking freedom through the pursuit of objects (temporary freedom gained through brief moments of happiness), while a very small minority choose to seek it through Self-inquiry (lasting freedom through elimination of ignorance).

Understanding God

Before introducing the various stages of devotion, it's helpful to review the three different definitions of God as they are shown in the Gita.

The first definition is **God as creator and cause of the universe**. This is the most common and elementary definition of God as understood by millions of devotees worldwide, regardless of their chosen religion. For those with this understanding, God has human attributes, exists outside of creation, and plays the role of arbitrator rewarding the "good" and punishing the "bad." God at this stage of understanding is a personal God providing emotional support and aiding in fulfillment of the devotee's wishes. This personification of God helps the individual to initiate a relationship with God and provides the mind with an object to meditate on.

Next, once an individual has developed some curiosity about the origins of the world, he or she is told that God is both the intelligence behind creation and the material itself. How does God make the creation out of itself? This was described previously using the analogy of the spider and the web. In the same way the web comes out of the spider but is not the spider, out of God comes the entire universe. At this stage, God is no longer a personal God but a universal God. The individual no longer looks for God in the heavens because God is to be found everywhere. Thus, **God as everything** is the second definition.

So, first, God creates the world and then, God becomes the world. God appears as the world in different forms, but God is not affected by any of them (just like the dreamer is never affected by the dream objects). In this way, God is the substrate that transcends all creation. This third definition of God is the most difficult, because in the third stage the individual understands **God as formless**, or non-dual consciousness.

None of the stages of understanding God negates the previous one, it simply completes more of the picture. This means we can appreciate God as a personal deity, as the totality of nature, and as the essence of all. This progression helps to explain the world's religions and why so few devotees ever realize the third definition of God—because it's not intuitive, it's difficult to understand, and it requires both a proper a guide and means of knowledge.

The Four Types of Devotees

Next, we turn to the various kinds of devotees.

> Arjuna, four types of people given to good actions worship Me—the distressed; the seeker of security and pleasure; the one who desires to know Me; and the one who knows Me. (Bhagavad Gita, 7.16)

There are four kinds of devotees, each characterized by their point of view, approach to the divine, discipline, and more. The first kind are described as "the distressed" or what is called in Sanskrit, an *arta* (from the word *arti,* meaning "sorrow, grief or trouble"). These are individuals who only seek a relationship with God when things are going badly for them. For these devotees, God is their last resort; someone to send an S.O.S. call to when they find themselves in desperate need of help.

The second kind of devotee is also worldly and is referred to as an *artharthi* (from *artha,* meaning "of secular value; material wealth"). This devotee is a seeker of security and pleasure, and views God as a sort of good luck charm. This devotee calls upon God to help them materialize what they most want and gain some control over that which is left to chance. They recognize there is always a factor that requires grace. For this devotee, God is like a partner and the relationship, transactional.

The problem with the first two worldly types of devotees described above is that God eventually takes away everything, including lent emotional support, objects and relationships. If your relationship with God is dependent on the things God provides, disappointment will eventually ensue.

The third and fourth kinds of devotees are said to be closest to

God and include those who desire to know God and those who already know God. The third kind of devotee is a *jijnasu* (from the word *jijnasa*, "to inquire") and doesn't seek favors from God but instead, wishes to know God by performing prayerful actions in order that God may reveal knowledge of itself. This devotee is different than the first two, who are desire-focused. This third type is what is referred to in Sanskrit as a *karma yogi*. They recognize that they are not in control of the outcomes of their actions and that whatever the results may be, they are provided by the grace of God. Karma yogis have a prayerful attitude and recognize that God has a hand in everything.

But of all the devotees, the fourth kind, the *jnani* (from the word *jnana*, "Self-knowledge"), is said to be closest to God because their devotion is absolute—meaning, there is no difference between the object of love (God) and the devotee who loves. The Self-realized devotee has developed an intellect subtle enough to realize that he or she is no longer separate from God. The other devotees are no different in body or mind, but haven't yet realized this important relationship. And what are the qualifications for realizing this unity with God? Discrimination, dispassion, discipline and an unstoppable desire for freedom. As Krishna says in the Gita, "Those who seek only me cross this maya." And while this may seem like just more faith-based religion, it becomes less so by the fact that to know God is to know the Self—the essence of who you are. It's what Nikhilananda means when he writes "in the final experience God and Truth are one and the same reality." In this way, devotion resolves into knowledge. As such, Self-realization is the highest form of devotion.

Of these four types are the Self-realized, who by their unwavering devotion are always united to me, and for who are very dear to me. (Bhagavad Gita, 7.17)

And even though the Self-realized devotee gets most of the praise from Krishna in the Gita, all devotees eventually cross the finish line, so that the first type of devotee becomes the second, the second will become the third, and the third will become the Self-realized.

The Five Stages of Devotion

Below are the five stages of devotional practice as they correspond with the different types of devotees, motives, stages of spiritual progress and associated practices.

Stage 1

The first stage of devotional practice is probably best defined as "rituals done to fulfill worldly desires." This stage includes the first two kinds of devotees who call on God as the creator for help with issues regarding security and pleasure, or when in need of emotional support. They reach out in hope that God might tilt the universe in their favor. Their devotion is childlike and is about supplicating God to get the results they're looking for. Because they aren't spiritually-motivated, they don't have any specific devotional practice. Any worship at this stage is informal, subjective and emotional. Selfish activity forms the first stage and it's where most *samsaris* fit in (individuals who totally identify with a sense of doership and the world as a source of happiness).

Stage 2

This stage includes the category of devotees who have some dispassion regarding the pursuit of worldly desires, are spiritually motivated and do certain spiritual practices for purification of the mind and eventual liberation. They also adopt a prayerful attitude that includes offering up all actions to God and accepting the results with gratitude. The devotee at this stage has evolved from doing selfish actions to selfless actions in the form of prayer and helping others in need (e.g., doing "God's work"). However, devotees in both stages 1 and 2 are still extroverted in their actions.

Stage 3

In this stage, the devotee now has interest in spiritual practices and makes an effort toward cultivating mental clarity. They might meditate on God based on a particular form. There is still duality in their view of God, but they are developing a deeper intellectual curiosity regarding the nature of God. At this stage, the devotee makes an effort to simplify their life, steady the mind through concentration practice and go inward.

Stage 4

Meditation on God continues but now includes the Total, as the devotee begins to understand that God is found in all people and objects. Their definition of God, therefore, has evolved from God as maker, to God as maker and material. They see God in what is perceived as both the "good" and "bad" about the world.

Stage 5

The final stage includes Self-inquiry (Vedanta). Worship is no longer worship in the traditional sense, but worship of knowledge based on the steps of Self-inquiry. This includes (1) devotion through hearing and subduing any personal opinions or beliefs until the teachings have been heard with earnestness (2) devotion through reflection and the elimination of any doubts and (3) devotion through assimilation by contemplating God as the formless essence of all. The devotee now sees God as both form and the formless, and no longer perceives God as separate from themselves.

Below is a summary of what has been discussed so far:

Stage	Devotee	View of God	Form of Devotion
Stage 1	*Arta, artharti*	God as creator and cause	Extroverted devotion that is child-like and about supplicating God to get desired results. No specific devotional practice. Worship is informal, subjective and emotional.
Stage 2	*Jijnasa*	God as creator and cause	Devotion is now introverted and includes a certain dispassion for the pursuit of wordly desires. Spiritual practices are done for purification of the mind and eventual liberation. Adoption of a prayerful attitude that includes offering all actions to God.
Stage 3	*Jijnasa*	God as creator and cause	Devotee continues to make effort toward cultivating mental clarity. Meditation on God is based on a particular chosen form. Most important, devotee has a deeper intellectual curiosity regarding the nature of God.
Stage 4	*Jijnasa*	God as everything	Meditation on God continues but now includes the Total (God as both maker and matter) and both the "good" and "bad" about the world.
Stage 5	*Jnani*	God as formless	Self-inquiry (Vedanta). Worship is no longer worship in the traditional sense, but worship of knowledge based on the steps of Self-inquiry. The devotee now sees God as both form and the formless, and no longer perceives God as separate from themselves.

The Steps Leading to Self-realization or Oneness with God

For the fifth stage of devotion, Vedanta outlines the necessary steps that lead to Self-realization. There is no skipping because each step prepares the individual for the next one. If skipping does occur, the devotee will find themselves going back in order to fill in the gaps of their understanding or to "re-qualify" if they find their practice faltering. For example, many westerners will approach Self-knowledge because they just want the answers to life's biggest questions. They understand the teachings from an intellectual point of view but lack the purification and steadiness of mind for the learnings to go in. Also, many times westerners enter Vedanta without any inclination toward understanding God, only to find themselves later interested in God because it's such an integral part to completing the puzzle.

Each step is traditionally called a *yoga*, meaning: discipline or practice. The word *yoga* in Sanskrit has several meanings. One definition is "a means to unite, join or connect with the destination." In this case, that destination is the Self/God. The three yogas prescribed to seekers are *karma yoga, upasana yoga* and *jnana yoga*.

The steps are defined as follows:

1. Karma yoga (purification of mind)

The steps to Self-knowledge represent the process necessary to reach liberation (moksha) or unity with God. Karma yoga (the "yoga of action") focuses on proper attitude and proper action. It's an external means for preparing for Self-knowledge that is applicable to everyday life, including work and the duties related to family-related duties. The benefit of karma yoga is a mind which is less bound by attachment and aversion. Binding likes and dislikes are a big obstacle to spiritual growth and therefore, require management as part of karma yoga. Karma yoga also helps establish a prayerful attitude toward life, therefore setting up the individual for the next phase—upasana yoga.

2. Upasana yoga (steadiness of mind)

Upasana yoga (the "yoga of spiritual discipline") is an internal means of preparing for moksha. It's the practice of gaining mastery of the mind through self-control and steadiness (also referred to as *raja yoga, ashtanga yoga,* or *samadhi yoga* based on Patanjali's eight-limb path). Upasana yoga is traditionally described as worship through meditation where the object of meditation is God, but concentration on a non-secular object such as the breath can also be used. Either way, the goal is to develop mental discipline. The four disciplines associated with upasana yoga include physical discipline (maintaining good health), verbal discipline (avoiding habits such as argument, gossip or idle speech), sensory discipline (avoiding that which holds sway over the mind or causes attachment) and mental discipline (concentration and mindfulness). In short, upasana yoga is about learning to live intelligently.

Both karma yoga and upasana yoga are dualistic since the devotee hasn't yet been introduced to Self-knowledge and still sees God as an entity separate from themselves. Nevertheless, Vedanta suggests that karma yoga and upasana yoga are compulsory because they are what help the devotee attain the four-fold qualification:

Discrimination—Clear vision or the ability to tell the difference between that which is true and that which isn't.

Dispassion—Seeing things as they are, free of projections. Dispassion isn't about having an aversion to all sense objects but instead, evaluating them intelligently. Neither is dispassion a "giving up," but more a "growing out of." It's the result of having Self-knowledge.

Discipline—The six-fold mastery of the sense organs and mind. The ability to (1) control the mind (2) control the senses (3) withdraw from sense objects (4) have forbearance (5) have faith in the teaching and the teacher and (6) concentrate. One "controls" the mind and senses through an understanding of our relationship with objects, including thoughts and feelings. Discipline also includes the upkeep of the body-mind (our instrument for achieving spiritual success).

Desire (for spiritual freedom) — The individual, frustrated by worldly experience and multiple failed attempts at finding lasting peace and happiness, instead, begins to look for it inwardly. With the gained understanding that true happiness can only to be found within, the desire for moksha becomes strong and the seeker dedicated.

Jnana yoga (Self-knowledge)

The next three steps leading to Self-realization (hearing, reflecting, assimilating), together, constitute jnana yoga (the "yoga of knowledge") or Vedanta. With jnana yoga, dualistic devotion (the idea that God and I are separate) is converted to non-dualistic devotion (the idea that God and I are one).

Up until now, the devotee has been cultivating a pure and steady mind in preparation for Self-knowledge. Without any of the previous steps, the mind will be too agitated and distracted by attachments and aversions to gain Self-knowledge.

3. Shravana (hearing)

The first part of jnana yoga is *shravana*, which involves hearing the teachings. Hearing (versus, just listening) can be a difficult task for most. We all have beliefs about who we are, about the world and how we got here that we've carried with us since childhood. Vedanta asks inquirers at this stage to sit down, remain quiet, and ask questions later. Needless to say, it requires an open mind because much of what Vedanta teaches is counterintuitive.

4. Manana (reflecting)

During the next part of jnana yoga, *manana*, the inquirer reflects on what they have heard and asks questions to clarify what, up until now, might have only been accepted based on faith. Inquirers are encouraged to eliminate every doubt until they see for themselves, the truth of the teachings. Vedanta can be challenging, not because of its seemingly encrypted content, but because ignorance is hardwired and tenacious.

5. Nididhyasana (assimilation)

The last step leading to Self-realization, *nididhyasana*, is the assimilation of the knowledge—and yet, it isn't final. There is no enlightenment certificate once you have some Self-knowledge because, as the wise like to say, eternal vigilance is the price of freedom! Nididhyasana can be summed up *as the constant meditation on the teachings until such a time the mind is convinced of its true nature.* This part of jnana yoga also includes the removal of any habitual tendencies which may still be lingering and inhibiting one's spiritual progress, such as certain binding vasanas.

To summarize the steps leading to Self-realization or union with God, (1) practice karma yoga for purity of mind, (2) practice upasana yoga for steadiness of mind, (3) find a teacher and gain Self-knowledge (jnana yoga) and (4) liberation/union.

Notes

1. From *Self-Knowledge (Atmabodha)*, as translated into English by Swami Nikhilananda and published by the Ramakrishna-Vivekananda Center of New York, Copyright 1946 & 1974, by Swami Nikhilananda.

2. "Spirituality" is a confusing term due to its association with soul-searching and the supernatural. According to Wikipedia, spirituality traditionally "referred to a religious process of re-formation which 'aims to recover the original shape of man,' oriented at 'the image of God.'" In modern times it has become a catchall for a "subjective experience of the sacred dimension," which "may involve belief in a

supernatural realm beyond the ordinary observable world." Vedanta sometimes puts itself in the category of spirituality in order to distinguish itself from faith-based religion. However, Vedanta is not easily categorized because it's a psychology, cosmology and theology and includes a fourth topic—non-dual consciousness. It's for this reason that it's probably best to just call it "Self-knowledge."

3. Swartz, James. *The Yoga of Love.* ShiningWorld.com, 2019. p.4.

Chapter 7

Is God Love?

Love is one of the most popular topics and yet, the least understood. A quick internet search on the question "What is love?" reveals a society not firmly grounded in reality. At a glance, the notion of love appears to be mostly based on beliefs, desires and hopes, which have inspired countless songs and other forms of artistic expression throughout the ages. "What is love?" is the one ballad we never seem to get tired of.

According to Christianity, love is an important attribute of God, appearing in both the Old Testament and New Testament. In John 4:8 it's stated that "God is love; and he who abides in love abides in God, and God abides in him." And Judaism refers to God's love in its prayer book when it states, "Deep is your love for us, O Lord our God, and great is your compassion..." (Gates of Prayer, 56). While the Muslims believe that without divine love there can be no human love because we are related to God through God's attributes. What all have in common is the belief that the path of real love is through God.

In spite of our wanting of and familiarity with love, most of us struggle to describe what it is. If you were to ask the random person on the street, they would probably make a few awkward attempts before concluding, "You just know it when you feel it!" So, love is an emotion. But as we all know, love comes in different forms. Certainly, unrequited love and compassionate love aren't the same thing, and even hatred can be categorized as a type of love (a distorted kind). So, before we ask if God is love, we need to take a closer look at this crazy little thing called "love."

It's probably obvious to most that object-oriented love is about getting and keeping. As members of a consumer-based society, we love our stuff. We love to acquire new stuff and when we no longer love it, we love to get rid of it. Object-oriented love can be thought of as a thing, person or situation that evokes pleasure. Thus, one definition of love is an attraction for an object that is a source of pleasure.

However, object-oriented love has its limitations and it's often due to these limitations that the pleasure an object makes us feel, turns into suffering. My love for an object can quickly dry up if the object no longer makes me happy. So, object-oriented love is conditional. For example, let's say I buy a vintage sports car because I like the full-sensory experience of driving in one of those old Ford Mustangs, including the way the car looks, the sound the V8 makes when it's revved, the way the car shakes when in idle, as well as the gritty smell of exhaust. I especially love it for its classic fastback style and the extra power I feel when I shift from second to third gear while getting on the freeway. However, I will no longer love my classic car when it begins to paint my driveway with oil, I'm unable to fix it without having to replace the entire engine, and when the cost of the repairs becomes more than what I originally paid for it! So, what I love, can quickly change to the opposite—repulsion.

Besides being conditional, object-oriented love is also like a time capsule. When I first bought my classic car, I washed it every weekend with specially formulated car suds, kept the vinyl well-conditioned, and finished everything off with a soft baby cloth. I also stored it covered in the garage, away from the elements. However, over the years the initial pleasure I felt for it slowly dissipated—even with everything still in good condition. I no longer admired its imposing racing stripe or the synthetic sheen of its seats. The loud engine became a nuisance and the smell of exhaust now made me nauseated. It was also taking up a lot of room in the garage. So, the vintage 1967 Mustang fastback was moved to the curb to collect dirt and rust while I looked for a buyer. What was before, my pride and joy began to look just like a heap of metal taking up space in my garage. The question is, what happened? Because nothing about the car had changed.

Due to our evolving attitudes, likes and dislikes, and the fact that familiarity breeds boredom, all objects eventually lose their luster. Fact: objects that seem interesting or sexy today, probably won't tomorrow. This is why the jiva must constantly be on the lookout for something more, better or different. We are always looking for ways to regain those initial few seconds of pleasure we got from an object the first time we experienced it (or as Starbucks Coffee likes to say, "That first sip feeling"). So, object-oriented love is fickle and at best temporary. I love my Starbucks Coffee up to the point the sugar-high and caffeine-buzz ware off — or until I get bored with it and start looking for something more, better or different.

Science agrees. According to authors Daniel Lieberman and Michael E. Long in their book *The Molecule of More*, we love the pleasure of anticipation — that is, the possibility of acquiring something unfamiliar and better — more than we love objects. The management of the "pleasure molecule" dopamine is how our brains reward us, or better stated, motivate us to acquire that which is not within close reach. However, once an object of desire is acquired and the object becomes a regular event, the pleasure-inducing effect quickly fades. The take-away is there's a difference between wanting something and liking it. From dopamine's perspective, getting things is more interesting than having things. Thus, if your mind is telling you "more, better, different," it's the dopamine speaking to you — a chemical.

What about romantic love? Unfortunately, romantic love isn't much different than object-oriented love. Both can be summarized as an extreme like or attachment. Mostly, we fall in love with someone because they offer some means to an end, whether it be companionship, security, validation, social status, money, sex or any combination of those. When those ends are no longer met, the hypnotic spell of romance quickly dissipates. Like all attachment to objects, relationships are also prone to maya's trick of projection and concealment (hence, the maxim, "love is blind"). When we fall in love, we mostly see only the perceived wonderful aspects of the person, while willfully ignoring the less-attractive ones. A relationship's romance is often put to the test when a couple decides to move in together and the little annoyances and character flaws that weren't obvious before, become highlighted and made obvious.

Furthermore, romance seldom survives the stress that comes with having children, paying a mortgage and taking annual family vacations to Disneyland—which is why marriage counseling has become a necessity for so many modern couples. Lastly, romantic love is reliably unreliable, because what you fall into you can just as easily fall out of.

Like object-oriented love, romantic love is also "dope." At the neurological level, dopamine is the instigator of romantic love. At some point, after several rides on the *maya*-go-round of romantic love that always seem to leave us at the same place we began, we realize that the seeming rewards of romantic love are just a big lie. That is why it's necessary for relationships to evolve in order to survive. Especially with long-term relationships, passion might need to become compassion as one's "little bundle of joy" changes in often unexpected ways.

At the neurological level, we can say future-oriented dopamine needs to transition to what science calls the "Here and Now" molecules (serotonin, oxytocin, endorphins and endocannabinoids). These molecules give us present-moment feelings of warmth and closeness toward other people. Thus, in order for a relationship based on romantic love to endure, passionate love must develop into what psychologists call *companionate* love—one that is mediated by the here and nows (H&Ns) and the present moment, versus by dopamine and the thought of some anticipated event (e.g., sex, marriage, financial stability, etc.). One is calm; the other is wild. One is the intertwining and gradual bonding through years of care, commitment and trust, while the other is brief and compulsive. One is in the now, while the other floats above reality.

Emotionally, with both object-oriented love and romantic love, there exists the hope that the object or person will make us whole and that it, she or he will complete us in a way that has eluded us up until now. This effort to make ourselves feel complete through objects is just another aspect of samsara. It's a misconception about the world that makes us extroverted looking for experience of wholeness "out there." Unfortunately, objects and relationships can't give love or make one complete, they can only elicit the *feeling* of love or completeness (more about that later), which is why, ultimately, they are unsatisfactory.

What about hate? Hate is also love, because in spite of its negative aspects, in a bizarre way it pleases one to hate. Hate may feel good on the surface but not so good inside where prolonged hate tends to fester and eventually sicken its host. Buddhists describe hate as like using your bare hand to throw a red-hot ball of iron at your enemy—what may or may not hit and hurt your target, will most certainly hurt you. Hate is a perverted kind of love—one that is twisted by anger or fear. Hate is also related to samsara with its ability to entrap and deprive us of real happiness.

Next is compassionate love. Unlike object-oriented love and romantic love, compassionate love isn't done for reasons related to "me." There may be those who would like to appear compassionate and want others to know they are compassionate in order to construct a certain kind of image, but real compassion doesn't involve the ego. In fact, compassionate love is closer to devotional love and both come from the same place.

In the Kaivalya Upanishad it says:

Experiencing one's own Self in all beings and all beings in the Self, one attains limitless awareness and not by any other means. (verse 10)

So, real compassion is a recognition of our shared nature with other sentient beings, and in particular, with those who are suffering or experiencing some kind of misfortune. When we witness someone suffering, it's natural for us to feel their pain. The origin of the word compassion is *compati* (Latin), meaning to "suffer with." If we stop to examine how compassion works, it seems to connect us to something greater and motivate us to take action. Real compassion is an authentic form of love, just as understanding, acceptance, giving, and friendliness are. Needless to say, these kinds of love are more closely associated with the warm, calm H&N neurological chemicals (oxytocin and endorphins) than with "more, better, different" dopamine.

You can tell authentic love from non-authentic love because there's a suspension of the wanting small-self—that part of you which is always scheming to get something back in return. For example, my friend has a neighbor who went on vacation without arranging for someone to take care of their cat while they were gone. The cat lost so much weight that its ribs began to show. So, my friend decided to feed the cat, not because she expected the cat to return the favor in any way, but out of empathy. The compassion she has for the cat is what moved her to reach out and help.

This ability to have and show compassion is natural to us and needn't be taught. Even the most hardened criminals, while they might not show compassion for other people due to their conditioning, are still capable of compassion—if not for anyone else, at least, for themselves.

Authentic forms of love are natural to us because they are an expression of our true nature, the Self. We love an object or a person because through it, or him or her, we temporarily discover some wholeness about ourselves.

Vedanta teacher Swami Dayananda writes:

> There is only one emotion which is real, which is your nature, and that is love—love as compassion, sympathy, understanding, giving, yielding, and as friendliness also. People often say, "You should be friendly, you should be accommodating, you should be this and that." It is not a question of should or should not; it is what you are. You do not ask a sugar crystal to be sweet; its nature is to be sweet. You are misled to have ideals without understanding that these are not ideals; these are you, your nature. It is a question of understanding; it is not to be commanded or demanded.[1]

The difference between object-oriented love and authentic love is that the former is experiential (because it requires an object) and only temporary, while the latter is unchanging, perfect satisfaction—fullness. One is dependent on an object, while the other is not. One is a fleeting feeling, while the other is the constant satisfaction that I am whole and complete. If I know that love is what I am, then I needn't seek out objects to find love because the source of all bliss/love is me!

As Dayananda further explains, "When all that is here is one whole, where is the question of your not loving? When you understand this, you have discovered love. There is nothing here but love." So authentic love is really just recognizing my essence as universal consciousness. But if that is the case, then what is the connection between love and the Self?

The logic goes like this: If reality is God, as non-dual consciousness, and if love exists (which it does), then there can be no difference between God and love. Therefore, to answer the question "Is God love?" — YES! God is love. God is love because love is its nature, just like it's sugar's nature to be sweet. And if love is God's nature, it must be ours as well because we are a reflection of the same original love.

In the Brihadaranyaka Upanishad, the sage, Yajnavalkya tells his wife:

> It's not for the sake of the husband, my dear, that the husband is loved, but for the sake of the Self. It's not for the sake of the wife, my dear, that the wife is loved, but for the sake of the Self. It's not for the sake of the sons, my dear, that the sons are loved, but for the sake of the Self.... (2.4.5)

Yajnavalkya is suggesting to his wife that it is the love for the Self that drives us to action. It is this love of the Self that serves as the foundation of all ethical laws. It is the reason why the Christian concept of the Golden Rule can be understood and appreciated regardless of affiliation with a religion or spiritual tradition. Ultimately, Yajnavalkya loves his wife because it pleases him to do so. Why? Because love is his nature. But in truth, he only ever loves (him)self because there is nobody else.

Author Edwin Faust writes in his book *We Can't Become Who We Are*:

> Whenever we love another, we love our Self as reflected in or projected onto that other. When we realize this, we can stop chasing love "out there," and rest in the love that is our true nature.

This is what the Indian sage Ramana Maharshi[2] considered the "highest devotion." When I say I love my wife, it's really just the Self pretending to love somebody else because we are both the Self—the one loving itself. Ditto, when I say I love my children. Love can only come from the Self. It can't come from objects because objects are inert, and it can't come from others because in reality, there are no others. That means the love I experience must be coming from me.

Thus, one of the crowning spiritual achievements—the "highest devotion"—is to discover that not only do I love, but that *I am love*. It's only by maya's power of reversal that the love that I am, appears to come from another. Therefore, if I love an object or a person, what I'm really saying is they elicit the feeling of love which belongs to me. The fact is the highest love is always reserved for (one)self, and what may appear to be narcissism is really love for God (God being none other than the Self).

You might wonder, "If I am love, then why don't I always feel love?" The love that you are is always there, it's just obscured by personal ignorance (avidya), conditioning and the gunas. When we experience hate, it's love perverted by rajas (projection) and tamas (concealment). We hate an object because it pleases us to indulge in hating it. Hate is often associated with an unconscious sense of helplessness, loss of power, a desperate need for validation, or some wanting of entitlement. On the other hand, we perceive authentic love when we are sattvic, which is why spiritual and devotional practice is useful because it helps purify the mind allowing us to cultivate love and therefore, feel closer to the divine—our actual Self. Just as loving another is really just loving one's Self (God), hating another is hating one's Self (God). So as followers of dharma with knowledge of the Self, we avoid hate—not because we ought to be good little boys and girls and only ever feel love for everyone all the time (which is impossible), but because we understand hate is just the Self masquerading as ignorance. Vedanta says "hate the sin not the sinner," because the sinner is just your own Self but in a different form. Our disgust shouldn't lie with the sinner but with ignorance. Even with ignorance, we must accept the fact that nobody chooses to be ignorant and suffer as a result. It's only due to their conditioning and the gunas that people are deluded, which is why forbearance is a virtue mentioned in the Gita.

As Swartz writes in his book *The Yoga of Love*:

It is helpful to see myself and everyone else as helpless fools or inert objects. I have good relationships with inert objects because I expect nothing of such things. I suffer fools gladly because I know they cannot be otherwise.

Notes

1. Dayananda, Swami. *Discovering Love*. Arsha Vidya Research and Publication Trust, 2009. p.50.
2. Ramana Maharshi was an Indian sage (1879–1950) who became Self-realized at a very early age and spent the rest of his life in meditation and encouraging others to seek freedom through Self-inquiry.

Epilogue

That Thou Art

You might be asking yourself at this point, "What do I have to gain from all this knowledge? How does it even make a difference?" The goal isn't to develop a keen understanding of eastern metaphysics, ancient Vedic cosmology and the minute nuances of describing the absolute, but instead to see that God and you are one. Intellectual pursuits have their place, but what we're going for is full unobstructed Self-actualization (a.k.a., "enlightenment")—a cognitive shift that totally reconfigures our view of the world and of who/what we are that isn't in conflict with reality.

From a practical perspective, God-knowledge helps remove that which inhibits us from seeing our true nature, which in turn allows us to live free of the negative psychological condition brought on by the misinterpretation of the world (the definition of samsara). Once God-knowledge is actualized, we no longer need to be always deceived by maya's tricks or relegated to endless suffering due to ignorance. We can begin to live in harmony with the world knowing we are part of something greater—not as some strange anomaly or quirky by-product of creation, but as the very essence of existence itself.

Because of this knowledge, I can know there is no distance between God and me and that any perceived difference between us is only an appearance (two separate, distorted views of the same original consciousness). Unfortunately, the further the perceived distance between God and me, the greater are my problems. So, it pays to have the right knowledge.

In the end, God as the creative principle (God 2) is for the jiva only. It's a way for the individual with its uniquely endowed intellect to make sense of the world and its role in it.

Any devotion to God 2 is really just about cultivating the right attitude that results in actions favorable to maintaining a sense of peace with oneself and the world. There needn't be anything "spiritual" about it since really, it's just an innate desire to be in harmony with what is, and at the same time, avoid any unnecessary suffering.

Devotion is often accompanied by the feeling of surrender when we set aside our striving small-self in order to feel closer to something greater—our true essence. How sweet it is to know we aren't the tiny, disconnected little dust mote we perceive ourselves to be, that in fact, we are both nothing and everything— both this apparent body-mind and the formless, spirit.

Neither is there is anything particularly remarkable about being a devotee. Devotees are simply individuals who know how to cultivate the proper mindset regarding life's circumstances. It just so happens that practices such as prayer, meditation, reading scripture and others that condition the mind toward a more harmonious relationship with God, are suitable to such a purpose.

In the end, the world and all which it inherit—"the cloud-capped towers, the gorgeous palaces, the solemn temples, the great globe itself"[1]—is like a dream where everything is constantly changing and nothing ever is what it seems. Upon close examination, we find that all the world is mithya—a passing show that "leave not a rack behind." So, in the final assessment, even God as creator must be dismissed. After all, God as a separate entity isn't the destination, you, the Self, are the destination—a destination that doesn't require any travel because that which you seek is what you already are. That thou art!

As I write these words, I stop to contemplate the thread that connects all of us like a string of pearls. As Krishna tells us in the Gita:

There is no cause superior to me. All this is woven in me like the beads on a string. (7.7)

It's all love because what else to feel once Self-realization sets in? What else to feel than utter reverence for God, the Self, this amazing universal principle that encompasses all things, including these very thoughts?

Notes

1. Our revels now are ended. These our actors, as I foretold you, were all spirits, and are melted into air, into thin air; and, like the baseless fabric of this vision, the cloud-capped towers, the gorgeous palaces, the solemn temples, the great globe itself, yea, all which it inherit, shall dissolve, and, like this insubstantial pageant faded, leave not a rack behind. We are such stuff as dreams are made on and our little life is rounded with a sleep (Shakespeare, *The Tempest* IV.i.148–158).

Addendum

Q&A

The following includes related topics that may have not appeared in any of the chapters, or that may have not been addressed directly.

Q: What is Vedanta?

"Vedanta" is a compound word in Sanskrit with *Veda-*, meaning "knowledge," and *-anta*, meaning "end." So, the first definition of Vedanta is the knowledge set down at the end of each of the four Vedas—sacred texts that originated in ancient India. It's at the end of these texts that the teachings of Vedanta, in the form of the written Upanishads, are unfolded. The second definition of Vedanta is "the knowledge that ends the search for knowledge," because once you understand the essence of who/what you are, there is no more searching. But in more general terms, we can define Vedanta as a means of knowledge that explains consciousness and removes a sense of limitation. Vedanta has a cosmology, psychology and theology, and includes a fourth topic—non-dual consciousness. Vedanta is sometimes referred to as the "science of consciousness" because it describes our experience in methodical and logical terms that explains away conflicting observations. Vedanta is also often referred to as Self-inquiry. However, "Self," in this case, doesn't refer to the I-sense (ego) but to non-dual consciousness, our true essence. Lastly, Vedanta proposes that what everyone is actually seeking is the Self and that the means to acquiring Self-knowledge is the removal of ignorance.

Q: Is Vedanta a religion or a philosophy?

Vedanta is not a religion or a philosophy, nor is it "spiritual" in the common use of the word. Vedanta is practical wisdom knowledge. It's not a religion because it's not based on beliefs but instead, logic and everyday experience. It's not a philosophy because it's not the idea of any particular person or school of thought, nor is it subject to modification because it already perfectly performs its function, which is to reveal the nature of consciousness.

Q: How does Vedanta define faith?

In the Vedantic tradition, faith is always faith pending one's investigation. The individual is encouraged to first listen, putting aside any beliefs or opinions. It's not until they have heard the teachings that they are encouraged to resolve any doubts. This is also why it's important to have a proper teacher and not just glean what you can from one's own interpretation of scripture.

Q: Isn't the Self, as the embodiment of Brahman, just another form of vitalism?

Historically, vitalism was science's pursuit to define a certain substance as the essence which enlivens the animate and differentiates it from the inanimate. For example, in the past it was thought that air was the special ingredient that enabled life. Later it was blood or the assumed substance *phlogiston*, which eighteenth-century chemists believed was the active agent in combustion. Another idea was that the elusive substance was electricity after experiments demonstrated an electrical current could make the severed leg of a frog twitch. Although the Self is sometimes described as "life force," it isn't vitalism because consciousness isn't a substance, action or an energy; nor could consciousness theoretically be transferred to an inanimate object (such as Mary Shelley's fictional Frankenstein's monster which drew inspiration from the then, popular interest in vitalism). "Life force" is best defined using the Sanskrit word *prana*, which is described as the five physiological systems including, respiration, evacuation, circulation, assimilation, and ejection. Nevertheless, without the Self, prana isn't possible. The actionless Self plays its role simply with its presence. Furthermore, when Vedanta says the Self is "consciousness embodied," it's meant to be figurative. The Self can't ever actually be embodied because, like space, it is limitless and permeates everything. In addition, the body is an object known to me (consciousness), which means instead of saying "consciousness is in me," we should say "the body is in me," because everything resolves into the Self. If it were otherwise, consciousness wouldn't be non-dual. Does space leave a pot once it is broken? No. Neither does it merge with other space because space is omnipresent and imbues everything. In the same way, consciousness never actually enters or leaves a body. Any appearance of it doing so is maya—the one appearing as the many.

Q: Isn't what you're calling the Self just solipsism?

According to Wikipedia, solipsism is "the philosophical idea that only one's mind is sure to exist." What solipsism postulates is that what we call the world—including all objects and the people—is a reality playing out in one mind—*my* mind. The error, in this case, would be to assume that the Self ("the one without a second") is solipsism. First, the Self is not the mind. The Self is actionless, non-dual consciousness; the screen on which the mind projects its thoughts. Secondly, Vedanta defines reality in three orders: (1) *paramarthika-satyam*, which is pure awareness (2) *vyavaharika-satyam*, which is transactional reality, and (3) *pratibhasika-satyam*, which is the jiva's own apparent experience. The first represents God 1's reality, the second represents God 2's apparent reality, and the third, the individual's. So, while experience is shaped by the individual's interpretation of transactional reality, God is still responsible for creating the world as we know it. Thus, Vedanta would say that while it's not true that all objects are the projection of a single mind (my mind), it is correct to say that all objects come out of the one consciousness and are dependent on the one consciousness for their existence. Therefore, the Self doesn't quite fit the definition of solipsism. Even if I were to somehow prove to myself that solipsism is true, the question would remain, what is it that is the substrate of the one mind's experience? What is it that knows this mind?

Q: How is it proven that God 1 is not the "void"?

God 1 cannot be the "void" because consciousness is not an experience, let alone an experience of nothingness. Experience is defined as consciousness plus a thought. The "void" that many people imagine experiencing after death is the non-experience of consciousness without any objects — like deep sleep. In the end, any idea of a void is just another superimposition on pure consciousness.

Q: Does Vedanta advocate for "intelligent design"?

While it's true Vedanta advocates an intelligent cause, it's not the same as the Christian concept of "intelligent design." For example, Vedanta doesn't suggest that God has a master plan and that human beings are the focus of that plan. Vedanta's vision of God takes into account all beings, not just human beings. Vedanta also has no qualms about evolution theory or how science describes the material world. However, Vedanta does propose that the universe is intelligently put together and maintained.

Q: Is Vedanta in agreement with science?

We must first acknowledge that while both Vedanta and science are interested in eliminating any and all obstacles to knowing the truth, they have different goals. Science tries to explain the origin, nature and processes of the natural world, while Vedanta aims to explain consciousness and remove a sense of limitation. Vedanta only explains the physically detectable universe insofar as it helps to meet the aforementioned objectives. Scientists today are mostly non-religious but accept the idea of an intelligent script that seemingly underlies how nature works. It's the pursuit of this intelligent script that motivates scientists to do research and write out mathematical formulae. While Vedanta and science might not describe the universe in the same terms, both agree that the universe exhibits an intelligence and that the material stuff of the universe can be described in terms of smaller components, forces, and information combining to form objects. Where Vedanta greatly differs from science is in showing that the ground of all experience is non-dual consciousness. Science and philosophy seem to say that only matter exists, while Vedanta says that ultimately, only consciousness exists. Vedanta has no problem with science as a means for understanding duality and the natural world, but would say that science's attempt to find consciousness *within* duality is made in vain. However much scientists search for the root of consciousness in the brain and other inert matter, they will never find it for the same reason a camera can never find itself in the photograph. Scientists will never find the source of consciousness because they can only ever verify their observations based on knowledge from the senses. Like the camera trying to find itself in the photograph, until scientists realize that what they are looking for is who/what they are, their search for consciousness will be elusive. With the exception of some internationally known and highly respected scientists from the last century (all nominated for or awarded the Nobel Prize),[1] most scientists generally prefer to avoid the murky world of metaphysics (an area of study often perceived as disreputable among their colleagues). And yet, it's a bit ironic that science has now reached a point where certain fundamental mysteries of the universe cannot be resolved without considering consciousness as a factor. This might eventually compel science to admit one day that the knowledge they are seeking has already been rigorously debated and known about for thousands of years, long before any scientific instruments. Astrophysicist (and self-proclaimed atheist) Adam Frank makes the point that as our scientific discoveries become more profound, we can no longer ignore how we find ourselves at the center of every experience as knowers of experience, and that it's this subjective perspective that must be taken seriously by science if we want to consider the biggest issues currently facing it.[2]

Q: Is devotion necessary for liberation (moksha)?

Devotion to God 2 traditionally comes in the form of belief, prayer, sacrifice, and ritual, while devotion to God 1 comes in the form of knowledge and contemplation. Is the former really necessary for moksha? Karma yoga, an outlook on life that can be practiced in a secular or non-secular way, is often prescribed to seekers as a means to mitigate the ego and correct their relationship with the world. Through karma yoga, the jiva is able to remind itself that they are not in control of the results of their actions and instead, relinquish the results to the Field (a.k.a., God). Karma yoga also helps the jiva to gain gratitude and appreciation for the impersonal intelligence that keeps the world going. So, it can be argued that some form of devotion is necessary for the purification leading to freedom. Without it, we may be unable to settle accounts with the world, even after gaining knowledge of the Self. In the end, any devotion to God is simply an intelligent approach to living that encourages a proper attitude toward life and the Field of Experience. It helps us to act wisely in accordance with God's laws and avoid suffering. That said, the liberated may still practice devotion to the creator

God knowing that ultimately, it's just the Self worshipping itself—a beautiful and satisfying practice.

Q: If God is everything, how does Vedanta explain the evil found in the world?

First, it's important to remember that God makes creation but doesn't become creation, just like the spider creates the web but doesn't become the web. From the perspective of God's creation, reality is neither good nor bad. Reality is value neutral. In fact, it could be argued that good and evil are only relative to an individual's point of view and conditioning. What is deemed "good" to one individual might not be to another (e.g., vegetarianism). In the end, evil is simply that which contradicts our likes and dislikes. Is it evil for a leopard to kill an antelope? Furthermore, because reality is a world that includes pairs of opposites, we can't have good without evil for the same reason you can't have sweet without sour or hot without cold. Vedanta teaches that the evil aspects of man are, in actuality, just the inevitable consequence of Self-ignorance. An "evil" person may be shown to be someone with a particular conditioning, influenced by the gunas, who has the erroneous belief that by doing certain actions that contravene dharma, they will be provided the freedom they aspire. However, without the gunas, there would be no jivas, let alone objects for awareness to be conscious of. In other words, there are impersonal forces operating that influence our every thought and action. So, Vedanta doesn't see evil as something innate to humans. If we must name a culprit it should be ignorance, not the person. Scripture often compares the unwise to children who, due to their inability to see the cause and effect of their actions, repeat the same mistakes over and over again. The wise say that the real test of devotion is to love God in all its forms. That said, Vedanta teacher, Sundari Swartz reminds us that Self-knowledge isn't a magic pill that

149

once taken, makes the jiva immune to all the evil in the world. We must still process the shock or trauma resulting from any exposure to evil. We can't always understand why things happen the way they do because as jivas, we can only look at what takes place in the apparent reality from within the framework of apparent reality. We can never grasp the bigger picture because our perspective is always, and will always be, limited in this maya. Sometimes, the only solace is to know that as the formless Self, I am never affected by evil. Krishna confirms this when he tells Arjuna:

> Weapons do not cut it, fire does not burn it, water does not wet it, wind does not wither it. This Self cannot be cut nor burnt nor wetted nor withered. Eternal, all-pervading, unchanging, immovable, the Self is forever the same. (Bhagavad Gita, 2:23–24)

Q: Is the concept of sin and sinner used in Vedanta?

No, because Vedanta would ask, who is it that's deemed the sinner? As Dayananda writes in his book *The Teachings of the Bhagavad Gita*:

> Condemning oneself as a sinner is the result of ignorance. Sins, wrong actions, belong to the actor, not to the Actionless [the Self]. If you discover yourself to be Actionless, where is your sin? By this knowledge you will transcend all sorrow; if you know what you are, the problem is solved. Just as a dreamer who has committed multiple murders in a dream is innocent upon waking, so too you are free from all sins when you wake up to the knowledge that you are actionless Awareness.... The fire of knowledge consumes every sin.[3]

The Gita confirms this:

Even if you are the most sinful of sinners, by the raft of knowledge alone you will surely cross over all sins. (4.36)

Once again, knowledge that I am the Self and not the doer is key. However, if we must put a definition to it, "sin" might be considered any action that goes against dharma (the universal laws governed by God) and as a result, accrues bad karma for the individual. In the Upanishads, sin is also sometimes the choice of words used to describe the impurities of the mind, which can be corrected, as suggested by scripture, through austerities (self-discipline; spiritual practices). In the same vein, Vedanta might interpret the Christian idea of original sin as the jiva's erroneous view that we are individual entities separate from God (the Self). Thus, original sin might be understood as the ignorance each of us is born with and which was passed onto to us from our parents, who learned it from their parents, and so on. The origin of the word "sin" means "to miss the mark," which is what we do when we believe we are a separate body-mind. As a result of our delusion, we suffer. Unlike Christianity, Vedanta says that ignorance (sin) isn't resolved by asking for redemption but instead, by removing the obstacles to knowing the truth. In the Gita, it is said that the Tree of Samsara (a metaphor for beginningless ignorance) can only be cut down by wielding the axe of knowledge. Thus, the ultimate solution to avoiding sinful acts isn't a question of seeking forgiveness and doing penance, but of understanding the essence of who/what you are. The wise don't grieve over past misdeeds because they recognize that the fault doesn't belong to them but to ignorance. This perspective on ignorance/sin is one of the defining points that sets Vedanta apart from religion. According to Vedanta, we are already free—we just don't know it. And yet to know it, we must first know the Self. And so it is written that "the fire of knowledge consumes every sin."

Q: Does Vedanta teach that we have a soul?

No, not in the sense that after death we go up to heaven where we are joined with deceased family members and friends. Most people envision the soul to be some ethereal version of their current person. They believe the soul to be "me" without the old worn-out body — which goes against the idea that our essence is the impersonal, universal Self. Therefore, "soul" (the embodied Self or *Atma* in Sanskrit) is sometimes used figuratively, but is not considered an entity with personal attributes. Vedanta teaches that there is no personality or aspect of a personality that survives death. Einstein, who didn't shy away from matters philosophical, once received a letter from someone imploring him to give an answer on whether or not a soul exists and if so, its development after death. In his reply he wrote, "Since our inner experiences consist of reproductions and combinations of sensory impressions, the concept of a soul without a body seems to me to be empty and devoid of meaning."[5] In other words, any existence of a soul after death would still require a body, senses, a mind capable of having an "I" thought, and a world with sense objects. So, in order to believe in a soul, you need to believe in that other definition of samsara — the transmigration of the soul from one incarnation to the next.

Q: What is Vedanta's perspective on death and the afterlife?

Any discussion of an afterlife, or whether one even exists or not, is a topic we can only speculate on. For some, the idea of having perpetual lives helps explain why some people are particularly apt at certain skills starting at a very early age (e.g., Mozart), and conveniently helps justify why some are born into misery while others are born into relative comfort. Life remains mysterious even for the enlightened. Vedanta doesn't claim to explain it all, just the part that matters most — the essence of who/what you are. However, with certainty we can say that if an afterlife does exist, even a celestial one, it would be just more mithya and therefore, something we should still want to seek freedom from (logically speaking, even heaven would have to have limitations because you can't have a "heaven game" without any rules). Nevertheless, Vedanta does offer up a theory for what happens when an individual dies.[6] Vedanta describes death in much the same way it describes deep sleep—with the subtle body being subsumed into the macrocosmic causal body. The theory goes that if the karma and vasana load[7] of the jiva (its psychology) are not resolved at the time of death, the vasana load will "travel" with the subtle body. This begins to sound a lot like the Christian idea of a transmigrating "soul." However, with the Vedic vision, the jiva's personality disappears with the death of the body. The subtle body is said to be eternal and may or may not transmigrate into another incarnation; but if there is an incarnation, it will not have the same personality. Memory of any previous incarnation is also erased (which is just as well, because who would want to inherit someone else's baggage and as a result, be born with a sense of regret or guilt). It is said that once a subtle body travels, it stays in seed form until the forces and laws that run the dharma field create the conditions for it to "sprout." Therefore, what is "reborn" is actually just the vasanas. The cause of perpetual rebirth (samsara chakra), according to the Vedas, is karma (action).

> Just as the body is nourished by the food and drink poured into it, by means of desires, contact, attachment, and delusion, the embodied one takes on, in succession, different bodies in various places according to its deeds. (Shvetashvatara Upanishad, 5.11)

It's the momentum of past deeds plus the identification with the body-mind that keeps the jiva firmly tied to the wheel of samsara (the relative world characterized by ignorance, desire and action). It's not until the jiva finds union with God (the

Self) that the cycle of samsara is broken. Similar to the concept of heaven and hell, reincarnation is a moot point for the Self-realized who already know they are not the doer. If I'm not the doer, why should I be concerned with what happens to the three bodies (gross, subtle and causal) after death? I am that which comes before birth and death and the three bodies. Ultimately, this is Vedanta's conclusion and what Krishna implies at the beginning of the Gita when he tells Arjuna:

> Although you speak words of wisdom, you grieve for those who needn't be grieved for. The wise grieve neither for the living nor for the dead. (2.11)

And from the Kena Upanishad:

> If a man knows Atman here, he then attains the true goal of life. If he does not know It here, a great destruction awaits him. Having realized the Self in every being, the wise relinquish the world and become immortal. (2.5)

According to Vedic tradition, "a great destruction" would be defined as endless cycles of birth and death, and worse, delusion (samsara). Once having recognized that the Self is present in every being, the wise, then, dismiss the world with its time-bound pleasure and suffering, and identify instead with that which is limitless and eternal.

Q: Does Vedanta's vision of God also include a heaven and hell?

Chapter 8 of the Gita explains in detail the afterlife trajectory of the four different kinds of devotees. It is also touched on in Chapter 15 while discussing the Tree of Samsara with its lower and higher branches. The concept of heaven and hell is mostly wrapped in karma theory and Hindu mythology. And while the topic is sometimes mentioned in Vedanta, it isn't emphasized. The reason is because for the Self-realized, the topic is moot. If in the end I discover that I'm not the doer, then I am that which is beyond any heaven or hell. Even if heaven and hell do exist, it's still just more mithya. Does that mean that the Self-realized are free to contravene dharma and do whatever they want? Maybe, but they have nothing to gain from doing so because they already know themselves to be whole and complete. Similarly, neither does Vedanta suggest that God sends individuals to a heaven or hell. For the most part, such religious beliefs are reserved for those who still don't qualify for Self-inquiry. We all like to imagine a special place where only pleasure is experienced and never any pain. But if we actually stop to examine our thinking on this, it doesn't make sense that such a place could ever exist. For one thing, to "travel" to heaven (assuming it's a physical location) you would need both a gross and subtle body. Even if your body were celestial, you would still be susceptible to pain, because only in deep sleep do we not feel any pain due to the absence of any experience of the body-mind. So pain is part of the package if you have any sentiency. Also, to assume heaven is only pleasure without pain isn't logical not only due to the law of opposites that says you can't have hot without cold or sweet without sour, etc., but because what is pleasurable can lead to attachment and ultimately, suffering. In other words, if heaven means becoming attached to it and never wanting to leave it, then heaven would no longer represent freedom—it would be binding, like any other coveted object. We may have also entertained the thought that once we arrive in heaven we will be closer to God. But if we were to arrive to such a place next to God, we would soon find many others like ourselves also interested in being close to God. Eventually, we would begin to compare our closeness to God with that of others. And that's all it would take to be subject to various degrees of suffering as we attempt to elbow our way toward God! Lastly, in Hindu mythology it's believed that even heaven has a time limit. The time limit is defined by how much good karma (*punya*) you have in your account. Once the good karma is spent, it's back to whence you came (sort of like having to return to the office after a wonderful vacation). And even though scripture talks about the heavenly abodes as being desirous, it doesn't say that entering any of them equates to spiritual freedom (moksha). The point is that wherever you go, you will eventually need to come back, because even heaven is still just more samsara. Therefore, any serious seeker shouldn't wish for heaven but instead, for a better future life in order to set themselves up for spiritual success—that is, to be given the necessary circumstances in order to gain and actualize the knowledge that sets one free.

Q: What about prayer?

Prayer is most commonly associated with religion and can be a useful practice, especially for situations where one finds it impossible to subjugate the senses through one's own efforts. In the Gita, Krishna admits:

> Indeed, Arjuna, the powerful senses violently carry off the mind, even of a wise man who makes great effort. The yogi endowed with discrimination, restrains them all and sits contemplating Me. His wisdom is steady whose senses are under control. (2.60–61)

Prayer is also useful for declaring one's intentions. Prayer expresses humility and a surrendering to God, recognizing that grace is needed in certain circumstances. Ultimately, prayer is just the Self communicating with itself. However, as jivas, it helps to have a fallback, particularly when overwhelmed by the gunas. Karma yoga, which encourages having a prayerful attitude, reminds us that we are an instrument of God. Prayer is also useful for having an ongoing conversation with the "higher intelligence," "universal force," "field of experience," "cosmic process" or whatever you wish to call it. As jivas, it recognizes that we are in a relationship with something much greater than what can be perceived by our limited view.

Q: Why do the sages say the world is perfect as it is and can't be any different?

From the standpoint of science, you can't take away any fundamental universal law without having the whole thing fall apart. If you want to have a world, everything must stay exactly as it is. If one day fire decided not to be hot or gravity decided to no longer be a force, we wouldn't have a universe anymore. Everything is interconnected, which is why we're now in such a precarious moment in human history as we willingly violate dharma and slowly commit ecological suicide. However, from a spiritual standpoint, the world seems to be the perfect setup for helping us arrive at what Vedanta calls moksha — liberation. To the jiva, the game of samsara is fixed so that if you lose, you lose and if you win, you still lose (i.e., all jivas eventually die and lose any perceived gains). This forces us to seek another route to freedom that doesn't involve being dependent on objects or relationships. It steers us away from being extroverts who are always seeking happiness "out there." I go into greater detail on this topic in my book Samsara: An Exploration of the Forces that Shape and Bind us.

Q: Does karma yoga mean saying "yes" to everything God sends us?

Even though God is everything, including both dharma (right behavior and social order) and adharma (the opposite), we are not obligated to say "yes" to everything God sends us. For example, we needn't accept every disturbing thought that enters our mind. We might take a disturbing thought and instead of identifying with it, give it right back to God. Another example might be if you find yourself in an abusive relationship, perhaps with a spouse or a boss. You needn't just sit down and take it because "it's God's will." So, while it's true that an aspect of karma yoga is the acceptance of life's ups and downs as grace, it doesn't mean that we shouldn't try to avoid adharmic situations. Sometimes karma yoga means applying proper action by using our God-given intellect to figure the best way out of a bad situation.

Q: Isn't Vedanta just more duality?

Yes. Ultimately, the teaching is just an instrument for realizing the Self. A common analogy used to show this is the use of a thorn to remove another thorn. Once the stuck thorn is removed, both thorns are thrown out. Vedanta removes duality. Once duality is removed, both Vedanta and duality can be thrown out and all that remains is the Self.

Q: To obtain Self-knowledge and therefore, gain union with God, must I study all the Vedic scriptures and learn Sanskrit?

No. The teacher, Gaudapada, in *The Mandukya Upanishad with Karika* clearly states:

> This Self cannot be attained through memorizing scriptural text, nor through discourse, nor through intense learning. It is only gained by the sincere seeker who wishes with their whole heart, to attain it. To such an individual, the Self reveals its true nature. (3.2.3)

Those who do study all the texts and learn Sanskrit mostly do so because they have a great love for Vedanta as a vehicle for knowing the Self. However, doing this is not a requirement for Self-realization. Obtaining Self-knowledge shouldn't be an academic endeavor but instead, done with the sincere desire to be free. That said, it does take discipline and perhaps, a little grace, which is only available to those willing to make an effort. So, Vedanta isn't an academic pursuit, but neither is it something you're going to learn in a weekend! It's a slow burn that includes: (1) purifying the mind through karma yoga (2) steadying the mind through concentration practice (3) hearing the teachings (4) resolving any doubts, and finally (5) assimilating the teachings. Vedanta requires preparation, long-term perseverance and the constant fine-tuning of one's understanding.

Q: How can I experience God?

You are already experiencing God because everything is God, including your body, your mind and all the objects you perceive. A wanting to experience God suggests that you are lacking something. Vedanta's message is there is nothing to be added to you because you are already complete—you just don't know it yet. If you are wanting to experience God, your problem is one of ignorance, not lack. The common misconception is that I can only experience God by having a mystical experience or through deep meditation (samadhi). But as this book has tried to show, God isn't a special enlightenment event. Such an understanding is too narrow and suggests that God is accessible to only a select few. Mystical experiences can be helpful for encouraging us to make the journey, but by themselves, provide only limited knowledge that quickly dissipates with time. Worse, such experiences can make us attached, causing us to suffer as we strive to recreate the same conditions. Profound meditation states may be good for obtaining a temporary sense of deep calm and for steadying the mind in preparation for Self-inquiry, but they don't make us much wiser. In fact, they can be misleading. How many times, as seekers, are we willing to admit we believed ourselves to be "enlightened" only to have our enlightenment vanish as soon as we got stuck in traffic or had to deal with any other of life's many inconveniences? Can we see God while stuck crossing the bridge to get to downtown, or only while sitting on a soft cushion at the end of a 10-day silent retreat? To experience God is to experience the Self, which is what you're doing all the time anyway. Each of us experiences the Self as "I am" all day, every day. Thus, instead of wanting to experience God, we should make the effort to *know* God. After obtaining the knowledge, our practice is simply to discriminate between what's true and what's not—no special enlightenment event required! While this might come as a disappointment to those who for years have firmly set up camp in the spiritual world, the truth is the truth. There is no other way out of this maya. Once you understand that you and God are one and that it's only ignorance that separates you from God, you can structure your life accordingly and begin to relax.

Q: How does someone who has obtained union with God look and behave?

"Enlightened" individuals come in all shapes and sizes and may or may not have the outward-facing spiritual demeanor that most assume they would. Each of us has been conditioned in different ways that preceded our interest in Self-knowledge/ God-knowledge, thus an enlightened person on the surface will appear no different than anyone else. The reason for this is because the only thing they have that the rest of us don't is Self-knowledge and the ability to apply it. They may be a calm and peaceful individual or due to their conditioning, an anxious one. They, like us, will have their own preferences for how to dress, interact with others, and spend their leisure time, etc., as long as it aligns with dharma. Leading a dharmic life comes naturally to the enlightened, as there are no longer any binding desires, fears and ambitions that drive them to carry out unwholesome actions. Knowing the mind and how the gunas corrupt it, they avoid activities that invite extreme tamas or rajas, and when tamas and rajas are unavoidable due to health or other issues outside of their control, they take the karma yoga attitude and find equanimity with the understanding that they are that which is beyond the gunas. The Gita provides numerous examples of how the wise behave. However, it's also important to know that the objective isn't to gain perfection in the human form (an impossible task in this lifetime and any lifetime due to the changing gunas). The wise may still get angry or become sad—after all, years (perhaps lifetimes) of conditioning do not just go away with a little knowledge. They may also still be vulnerable from time to time to maya's old tricks. Deeply entrenched vasanas called *samskaras* sometimes appear out of nowhere with no warning. But to be truly free one must be free to be angry, sad, disappointed, etc., as well as happy and peaceful. Again, perfection of the jiva is not the goal. The goal is freedom from and for the jiva, which means freedom *from* identifying with the body-mind and one's innate programming. The wise gladly acknowledge they are not the doer and instead, choose to identify with pure consciousness. The difference, again, is knowledge. Like a super power, once the knowledge is applied, samsara disappears. People often like to imagine that the enlightened have some kind of magic or special attribute that the rest of us don't, but the knowledge, once learned and applied, *is* the magic; and while it doesn't enable one to move through walls, read people's minds, or visit celestial whereabouts, it does something a whole lot better: remove the suffering associated with ignorance.

In the darkness which sleep all beings, the wise one is awake. Where other beings are awake, it's darkness for the wise one who sees (Bhagavad Gita, 2.69).

Notes

1. Some of the physicists who took an interest in the teachings of the Vedas include: Erwin Schrodinger, Werner Heisenberg, Niels Bohr, Robert Oppenheimer, and David Bohm.
2. Frank, Adam. "Thinking thresholds: Is science the only source of truth in the world?" *Big Think.* https://bigthink.

com/hard-science/science-truth/

3. Dayananda, Swami. *The Teachings of the Bhagavad Gita*. Orient Paperbacks, 2005. p.71.

4. Swartz, James. *The Yoga of Love*. ShiningWorld.com, 2019. p.121.

5. Einstein, Albert. *Albert Einstein, the Human Side: New Glimpses from His Archives*. Princeton University Press, 1981. p.40.

6. For a full description of death and the hereafter according to Vedic scripture, see Brihadaranyaka Upanishad, part 4, chapter 4 or Chandogya Upanishad, part 5.

7. According to karma theory, a person's future birth is determined by the intense (binding) desires they still hold at death. Desire (kama) leads to action (karma), which creates a tendency (vasana) for wanting more of the same. This wanting then perpetuates into a future life where it makes the individual assume a body in an environment where he or she will have an opportunity to fulfill their desires. This cycle of rebirth is most commonly described as "samsara." However, once Self-knowledge has been realized, any remaining vasanas will eventually dissolve because there is no longer a doer to sustain and identify with them. Hence, the cycle is broken. In regard to karma, a Self-realized individual will still need to exhaust any remaining karma that was accumulated before Self-realization. This residual karma (*prarabdha karma*) is sometimes compared to the blades of a moving fan which continue turning even after the fan has been powered off.

About Vedanta

To the outsider, Vedanta and the teaching of non-duality may appear an elaborate fabrication—just another story cooked up by a people from a bygone era. After all, in a world full of spiritual charlatans who like to feed on the desperation of people seeking an escape from their suffering, it's prudent to be skeptical and not just dive in head first. "Choose your story wisely," is one of the best pieces of advice to anyone at any age.

But there's something different about Vedanta and what it teaches. As an ancient wisdom tradition, Vedanta has the unique status of not being a religion or a philosophy. Even "spirituality" doesn't seem to fit it. Vedanta is closer to a science and yet, in addition to having a psychology and cosmology, it has a theology. Perhaps, it's best to simply define it as *a unique means of knowledge that explains consciousness and removes a sense of limitation.*

Vedanta helps to solve the problem of ignorance. Because of ignorance, an individual views a universe of name and forms and takes the body-mind to be oneself. This creates the illusion of life being a duality that includes pairs of opposites such as good and evil, birth and death, pleasure and pain, and light and darkness. Vedanta contends that the world comes out of consciousness, the essence of who/what we are, and that our misidentification with objects is the cause of our suffering. That we are pure consciousness means we are eternally free and limitless. Once this truth is known, the illusion of duality disappears and the universe reveals itself to be benign.

Vedanta provides a systematic means called Self-inquiry that progressively reveals the nature of this truth and ultimately, alleviates sorrow. Because Vedanta is an objective analysis of our experience, it is indifferent to historical, cultural or personal opinion. One of its most important aspects, like all great knowledge-based traditions, is that it is universally applicable.

The teachings of Vedanta are counterintuitive, so one's first exposure to it most likely will inspire more skepticism than faith. But faith is only meant to be provisional. In Vedanta, faith is always taught as faith pending your own investigation, much like a scientific formula before putting it through the rigor of application. In Vedanta, these forms of proofs are called *prakriyas* or methods of Self-inquiry.

When one is first introduced to chemistry or physics, it also feels implausible to learn about something not immediately recognizable. This is why scientists rely on empirical evidence, because otherwise it's all just theory or worse, elaborate conjecture. Science never asks you to believe, instead it provides you with the tools with which to draw your own conclusion. When hundreds of scientists are able to follow the same process and draw the same conclusion, it's no longer just a hypothesis.

In science, there are certain inarguable principles like gravity or the speed of light. We may not understand how these phenomena come to be, but we cannot deny their existence and should we have the interest, know that we can retrace the steps of other scientists in order to investigate and prove to ourselves their validity. For this reason, we say science is a process for discovering objectively verifiable facts. In much the same way, the teachings of Vedanta appear mysterious and encrypted until we take the necessary steps to understand it.

Any proper teaching includes a methodology—a sequence of small learning increments that slowly build up to more complicated and subtle concepts. As such, Vedanta's methodology begins with the basic premise that as conscious beings we feel limited, and it ends with the enigmatic Sanskrit phrase, *tat tvam asi*—"You are that." As curious students, eager to have all the answers, we might want to jump to the end of the teaching and then go back to see where there are gaps in our understanding. Many "Neo-Advaita" teachers, knowing what seekers really want, will deliver the goods first without providing a proper teaching. It's for this reason that even today, there's much misunderstanding around the concept of enlightenment, and why the best Vedanta teachers will often go out of their way to debunk enlightenment myths.

Vedanta teaches two distinct practices or *yogas*. A *yoga* is a discipline or means of preparing the mind in order to help make the truth accessible. Vedanta recommends various yogas such as meditation to help steady the mind, but mostly focuses on *karma yoga* and *jnana yoga*. *Karma yoga* (the yoga of action) is a preparation for jnana yoga (the yoga of Self-knowledge). The karma yoga teaching is relatively straightforward, and yet many Westerners initially don't appreciate its value and will choose to bypass it, only to find out later they need to come back to it to complete their practice. The reason for this is because it involves our relationship with God. Needless to say, most Westerners who come to Vedanta seeking answers to life's biggest questions aren't interested in God. In fact, it might be God (the biblical one) they're trying to run away from! Nevertheless, God-knowledge is an important part of the Vedanta equation and in the end, becomes difficult to ignore.

God or "Ishvara," as it is used in Vedanta, is responsible for creating, maintaining and recycling the Field of Experience. Ishvara provides the results of our actions and is the keeper of *dharma*—the universal physical, psychological and moral laws. Unlike some religions, Vedanta doesn't portray God as an old man sitting in the heavens rewarding the "good" and punishing the "wicked." Instead, it shows God as the force behind all nature. God isn't so much an entity, as it is a principle—like gravity. For this reason, Vedanta doesn't suggest one *believe* in God. Vedanta asks, "Why believe in God when you can *know* God?" In other words, God needn't be a story.

The word *karma* means action and the result of action. What karma yoga teaches is to practice whatever you do as an offering to the Field or Ishvara—whether it be preparing food for a meal or brushing your teeth. Karma yoga also teaches that we are not responsible for the results of our actions—Ishvara is. We accept all results, good and bad, as *prasad* or a gift from God (God's grace). Sometimes prasad arrives as something delightful to encourage us along our journey, and sometimes those gifts may come in a negative form as a lesson meant to correct our understanding. In short, karma yoga is about having "God on your mind." More than just a practice, karma yoga is an attitude that promotes gratitude and acceptance. The effects are two-fold: First, it relieves stress because we are no longer looking at just the negative aspects of life or believing it's all up to us. Second, it softens the ego and diminishes its fallacious argument that it's an independent entity (more often than not, it's our egos that get in the way of our understanding). Most importantly, without the sincere practice of karma yoga, jnana yoga becomes a cold intellectual exercise. So, karma yoga is necessary, even if you have to come back to it later.

Jnana yoga, or Self-inquiry, is a three-stage process: hearing (*shravana*), reasoning (*manana*) and actualizing (*nididhyasana*). Notice that the first stage, *shravana*, is hearing (not listening). In order to hear what someone is telling us, we must first silence our own commentary so that we can understand and consider what's being said. During the *shravana* stage we temporarily subdue our beliefs and opinions until we hear what Vedanta has to teach. The *manana*, or reasoning stage, involves comparing the teachings with our own experience and resolving any doubts. The last stage is *nididhyasana*. During this stage we regularly contemplate the teachings and let the knowledge work on us. *Nididhyasana* is an on-going practice because the cost of freedom from ignorance means constant vigilance.

Part of Vedanta's ability to deliver *moksha* or liberation is in its use of a proven methodology. If Vedanta had a curriculum, the course outline might look something like this:

Vision

As an introduction to Vedanta we'll learn about its origin and find out what Vedanta is, what it offers, and what it is not.

Motivation

In this next segment we'll discuss the three human pursuits and humanity's fundamental problem. Other topics will include the limitations of object-oriented happiness and the qualities of *samsara*.

Preparation

As preparation for Self-inquiry we will start off by asking "What is enlightenment?" and also debunk several enlightenment myths. We will introduce a few traditional teachings, namely the location of experience and happiness, followed by a definition of non-duality. We will go over the qualifications for and obstructions to moksha (liberation), and end with dharma and the "value of values."

Self-Inquiry

At the heart of Vedanta is Self-inquiry or jnana yoga. We begin the process by identifying, as an individual, what I am not (*neti-neti*). Discussion will include the difference between subject and object, the five sheaths, the three states of experience, and how Vedanta defines what is real. Next, will be an in-depth look at awareness — the essence of everything. We will define existence, as well as define that most interesting of human emotions — love. Lastly, we will introduce the next section with an explanation of the three orders of reality.

God (*Ishvara*)

No spiritual teaching is complete without a discussion on the relationship between individuals, the world and God (the creator, sustainer and destroyer of the world). In this section of the course, we'll share Vedanta's view of God and why it's valuable to have God-knowledge. We'll discuss the Field of Experience, as well as maya and dharma. We will finish the section with an explanation of karma yoga and why it's preliminary to Self-knowledge.

World (*Jagat*)

To continue the topic of God (Ishvara), we will take a look at Ishvara's creation, as well as its constituents, namely the five elements and the *gunas*.

Individual (*Jiva*)

To round out our trio, next we'll move to the jiva (person, being, or conscious life form). The jiva is explained in the context of the three bodies (gross, subtle, and causal). The concept of karma will be examined in detail, as well as other topics such as free will, birth and death, and the difference between a person and other life forms. We'll finish by talking about jiva's unique relationship with Ishvara. .

Purification

Purification is about preparing the mind for Self-inquiry and sustaining clarity by leading a healthy lifestyle. We'll discuss various yogas or disciplines, including *raga-dvesha* (likes-dislikes), *upasana yoga, triguna vibhava yoga,* and *bhakti yoga.*

Scripture

While we frequently refer to scripture, in this final phase we will reveal the meaning behind some of the more important phrases and texts of Vedanta including the *mahavakyas* or "great statements." We will also identify and summarize some of the more important Vedantic texts.

As seen by the example of a curriculum, there is a sequence to how Vedanta and the truth is unfolded. It's by this process that—if both student and teacher are qualified—there are no questions left unanswered and the nature of experience is explained. As mentioned from the beginning, Vedanta is a complete teaching that includes a psychology (the person), a cosmology (the world), and a theology (God). All of these topics resolve into a fourth factor that Vedanta reveals as the substrate to all experience—non-dual awareness.

How will we know the effects of Vedanta after obtaining and actualizing its knowledge? The primary evidence is that once we have understood the teachings well, all further seeking ceases. Our appetite for new philosophies and spiritual experiences dissipates. In short, we feel satisfied—full. We will also see old attachments and tendencies fall away—sometimes effortlessly, sometimes with much work. Life will still be appreciated for what it is, but no longer chased after or feared.

Acknowledgements

The teachings included in this book are not mine, I've only organized them around a common theme (perhaps, inadequately). They all belong to a long and venerable wisdom tradition that dates back millennia. Thus, the list of acknowledgements here should be much longer! That said, I'd like to express a big "thank you" to the usual disseminators of non-dual wisdom who have helped make the teachings of Vedanta clear and comprehensible to a Western audience, in particular, James and Sundari Swartz. James's book *The Yoga of Love* afforded me with an invaluable understanding of non-dual devotion, while Sundari's written satsangs provided additional inspiration for many of the chapters. I would also like to thank Swami Paramarthananda, whose commentary on *Tattva Bodha* informed much of Chapter 3 and the section on cosmology. Swami Paramarthananda of Chennai, India, is one of the great living proponents of traditional Advaita Vedanta. I would also like to acknowledge the writings of Swami Dayananda, which provided the initial ideas for the chapter on "One Great Order" and much more. And also, the writings of Swami Nikhilananda of the Ramakrishna Mission, who during the middle part of the twentieth century published a remarkable four-volume translation and commentary, edited by Joseph Campbell, on the principal Upanishads. I often turned to his books when I needed to fill in any missing gaps or resolve doubts regarding my understanding of certain verses. Lastly, I would like to give thanks to Ishvara who graced me with the desire and means to seek out the "secret knowledge."

Daniel McKenzie
April 2022

Bibliography

Abdin, Amira Shamma. *Love in Islam.* European Judaism: A Journal for the New Europe. vol.37. No. 1 (Spring 2004). Berghahn Books.

Aczel, Amir D. "Why Science Does Not Disprove God." *Time,* April 27, 2014, https://time.com/77676/why-science-does-not-disprove-god/

Al-Khalili, Jim. *The World According to Physics.* Princeton University Press, 2020.

Alpert, Mark. "Can Science Rule Out God?" *Scientific American,* December 23, 2019, https://blogs.scientificamerican.com/observations/can-science-rule-out-god/

Bryson, Bill. *A Short History of Nearly Everything.* Crown, 2003.

Campbell, Joseph. *Myths of Light: Eastern Metaphors of the Eternal.* Joseph Campbell Foundation, 2018.

Davies, Paul. *The Fifth Miracle: The Search for the Origin and Meaning of Life.* Simon & Schuster, 2000.

____*The Goldilocks Enigma: Why Is the Universe Just Right for Life?* Mariner Books, 2008.

____*The Mind of God: The Scientific Basis for a Rational World.* Simon & Schuster, 1993.

Dayananda, Swami. *Discovering Love.* Arsha Vidya Research and Publication Trust, 2009.

____*Isvara in One's Life.* Arsha Vidya Research and Publication Trust, 2019.

____*Need for Cognitive Change.* Arsha Vidya Research and Publication Trust, 2019.

____*The Need for Personal Reorganization.* Arsha Vidya Research and Publication Trust, 2019.

____*The Bhagavad Gita Home Study Program.* Arsha Vidya Research and Publication Trust, 2019.

____*The Teachings of the Bhagavad Gita.* Orient Paperbacks, 2005.

Einstein, Albert. *Albert Einstein, the Human Side: New Glimpses from His Archives.* Princeton University Press, 1981.

Faust, Edwin. *We Can't Become Who We Are: Commentaries on Ramana Maharshi's "Upadesha Saram."* ShiningWorld. 2018.

Frank, Adam. "Thinking thresholds: Is science the only source of truth in the world?" *Big Think.* https://bigthink.com/hard-science/science-truth/

Gleiser, Marcelo. "Isaac Newton's life was one long search for God." *Big Think.* https://bigthink.com/13-8/isaac-newton-search-god/

Kahneman, Daniel. *Thinking, Fast and Slow.* Farrar, Straus and Giroux, 2011.

Kuhn, Robert Lawrence. "Forget Space-Time: Information May Create the Cosmos." *Space*, May 23, 2015, https://www.space.com/29477-did-information-create-the-cosmos.html

Lieberman, MD, Daniel Z; Long, Michael E. *The Molecule of More.* BenBella Books, Inc. 2018.

Mackay, Rory. "Free Will and The Three Orders of Reality." *Unbroken Self.* https://www.unbrokenself.com/action-free-will/

____"Jiva is Just a Thought." *Unbroken Self.* https://www.unbrokenself.com/jiva-is-just-a-thought/

McKenzie, Daniel. *The Wisdom Teachings of the Bhagavad Gita.* Self-published. 2020.

Nikhilananda, Swami. *The Bhagavad Gita: The Song of the Lord.* Ramakrishna-Vivekananda Center of New York, 1944.

____*Self-Knowledge (Atmabodha).* Ramakrishna-Vivekananda Center of New York, 1946 & 1974.

____*The Upanishads: A New Translation.* Volumes 1 - 4. Ramakrishna-Vivekananda Center of New York, 1949–1959.

Nurse, Paul. *What Is Life?: Five Great Ideas in Biology.* W.W. Norton & Company, 2021.

Oreskes, Naomi. "If You Say 'Science Is Right,' You're Wrong." *Scientific American.* https://www.scientificamerican.com/

article/if-you-say-science-is-right-youre-wrong/

Paramarthananda, Swami. *Commentary on 'Drg Dryshya Vivika'*. Arsh Avinash Foundation, https://arshaavinash. in/index.php/download/drg-drsya-viveka-by-swami-paramarthananda/

_____*Does God Exist?* Arsh Avinash Foundation. https:// arshaavinash.in/index.php/download/does-god-exist-by-swami-paramarthananda/

_____*The Relevance of God*. Swami Paramarthananda Lectures. http://spiritualsathya.blogspot.com/2017/10/god-centred-life-2422017.html

_____*Tattva Bodha*. Arsh Avinash Foundation. https:// arshaavinash.in/index.php/download/tattva-bodhah-swami-paramarthananda/

Schmidt, Ted. *Self-Knowledge: The King of Secrets*. Two Harbors Press, 2016.

Swartz, James. *Inquiry into Existence: The Lamp of Knowledge*. ShiningWorld, 2019.

_____*The Yoga of Love*. ShiningWorld, 2019.

Pattanaik, Devdutt. *Indian Mythology: Tales, Symbols, and Rituals from the Heart of the Subcontinent*. Inner Traditions, 2003.

Tippett, Krista. *Einstein's God*. Penguin Publishing Group, 2010.

Venugopal. D. *Vedanta: The Solution to Our Fundamental Problem*. Bharatiya Vidya Bhavan, 2012.

Viglietti-Swartz, Isabella (Sundari). "Facts about Jiva and Moksa." *ShiningWorld*. https://www.shiningworld.com/facts-about-jiva-and-moksa/

_____"Free Will and the Isvara Metaprogram." *ShiningWorld*. https://www.shiningworld.com/free-will-and-the-isvara-metaprogram/

_____"No Way to Stop Hate." *ShiningWorld*. https://www.shiningworld.com/no-way-to-stop-hate/

_____"The Self is Consciousness." *ShiningWorld*. https://www.shiningworld.com/the-self-is-consciousness/

____"When Does Karma Yoga Not Work?" *ShiningWorld*. https://www.shiningworld.com/when-does-karma-yoga-not-work/

____"Why Everyone Needs God." *ShiningWorld*. https://www.shiningworld.com/why-everyone-needs-god/

Zimmer, Heinrich. *Myths and Symbols in Indian Art and Civilization*. Princeton University Press, 1946.

MANTRA
BOOKS

EASTERN RELIGION & PHILOSOPHY

We publish books on Eastern religions and philosophies. Books
that aim to inform and explore the various traditions that began in
the East and have migrated West.
If you have enjoyed this book, why not tell other readers by
posting a review on your preferred book site.

Recent bestsellers from MANTRA BOOKS are:

The Way Things Are
A Living Approach to Buddhism
Lama Ole Nydahl
An introduction to the teachings of the Buddha, and how to make use of these teachings in everyday life.
Paperback: 978-1-84694-042-2 ebook: 978-1-78099-845-9

Back to the Truth
5000 Years of Advaita
Dennis Waite
A demystifying guide to Advaita for both those new to, and those familiar with this ancient, non-dualist philosophy from India.
Paperback: 978-1-90504-761-1 ebook: 978-184694-624-0

Shinto: A celebration of Life
Aidan Rankin
Introducing a gentle but powerful spiritual pathway reconnecting humanity with Great Nature and affirming all aspects of life.
Paperback: 978-1-84694-438-3 ebook: 978-1-84694-738-4

In the Light of Meditation
Mike George
A comprehensive introduction to the practice of meditation and the spiritual principles behind it. A 10 lesson meditation pro-gramme with CD and internet support.
Paperback: 978-1-90381-661-5

A Path of Joy
Popping into Freedom
Paramananda Ishaya
A simple and joyful path to spiritual enlightenment.
Paperback: 978-1-78279-323-6 ebook: 978-1-78279-322-9

The Less Dust the More Trust
Participating in The Shamatha Project, Meditation and Science
Adeline van Waning, MD PhD
The inside-story of a woman participating in frontline meditation
research, exploring the interfaces of mind-practice, science and
psychology.
Paperback: 978-1-78099-948-7 ebook: 978-1-78279-657-2

I Know How To Live, I Know How To Die
The Teachings of Dadi Janki: A warm, radical, and life-affirming
view of who we are, where we come from, and what time is calling
us to do
Neville Hodgkinson
Life and death are explored in the context of frontier science and
deep soul awareness.
Paperback: 978-1-78535-013-9 ebook: 978-1-78535-014-6

Living Jainism
An Ethical Science
Aidan Rankin, Kanti V. Mardia
A radical new perspective on science rooted in intuitive awareness
and deductive reasoning.
Paperback: 978-1-78099-912-8 ebook: 978-1-78099-911-1

Ordinary Women, Extraordinary Wisdom
The Feminine Face of Awakening
Rita Marie Robinson
A collection of intimate conversations with female spiritual
teachers who live like ordinary women, but are engaged with their
true natures.
Paperback: 978-1-84694-068-2 ebook: 978-1-78099-908-1

The Way of Nothing
Nothing in the Way
Paramananda Ishaya
A fresh and light-hearted exploration of the amazing reality of
nothingness.
Paperback: 978-1-78279-307-6 ebook: 978-1-78099-840-4

Readers of ebooks can buy or view any of these bestsellers by
clicking on the live link in the title. Most titles are published in
paperback and as an ebook. Paperbacks are available in traditional
bookshops. Both print and ebook formats are available online.

Find more titles and sign up to our readers' newsletter at
http://www.johnhuntpublishing.com/mind-body-spirit.
Follow us on Facebook at https://www.facebook.com/OBooks
and Twitter at https://twitter.com/obooks.